Old Time Cattlemen and Other Pioneers of the Anza-Borrego Area

by
Lester Reed

PRINTED BY
DESERT PRINTERS, INC.
PALM DESERT, CALIF.

Dedication

He was a man whose code of honor was founded mainly upon loyalty, truth, honesty, sober dependability, the keeping of faith, and the word of God. The nearest anyone could have come to knowing how many friends he had would have been to know how many people were acquainted with him. As a boy of 14 years, he came from Comanche County, Texas, to Southern California, in 1867, taking his turn the same as the men, driving one of the ox teams in a covered wagon train, helping to drive a small herd of cattle, and taking his turn standing guard at night. This wagon train crossed the Colorado River at Yuma, Arizona, and continued to follow the Butterfield Stage Route by way of Carrizo Creek and Vallecito. His name was Quitman Reed, and to him, my wonderful father, I dedicate this book.

Acknowledgements

To all old-timers whose names I have mentioned in these pages I wish to express my appreciation. As a boy and young man, I knew just about all of them, and among these old-timers were relations on both sides of my family—the Tripps on my mother's side, and of course, the Reeds on my father's side.

To Mrs. D. A. Forsythe, of Dundas, Ontario, Canada, I am very grateful for her being the one who awakened in me the idea that I must not delay any longer in getting started with my writing, just because I did not feel myself qualified.

To Vina Reed, I feel that I must express my appreciation, for it was she who furnished me with the copy of the John Taylor Diary of the trip from Texas to California with ox-teams and covered wagons in 1864.

To Judd Tripp I am indebted for the tape recordings I have from him concerning his experiences in the Anza-Borrego Desert.

To Sylvester ("Sal") Biles and his wife, Treasure, I am thankful for the help they gave to me with photos and relating again to me experiences at Clark Lake, Coyote Canyon, and Borrego Valley. I am most grateful for their being unusual friends.

To Howard Bailey and his wife, Lola, I must say "thank you" and hope to further express my appreciation of the fine photos and tape recordings that have helped so much in referring to happenings in the desert areas before the coming of surfaced roads.

To Karl V. Bennis who helped to start the transition of the Anza-Borrego Desert from a land of travel by ox-team, wagons drawn by horses and mules, the prospectors with their faithful burros, the saddle and pack animals of the cowboys, to a land of travel by jeep, I cannot find enough words to express my appreciation of the many hours of his companionship in the Anza-Borrego Desert. In addition, I must say "thanks" for the photos furnished me for these pages.

To Mr. and Mrs. Arthur Cary, who still reside at La Puerta (San Carlos Pass), I am very grateful for the reproductions of photos, including a reproduction of the transfer of title to the lands at La Puerta (La Porto) from Pesqual to F. S. Clark; the reproduction of Fred Clark and his autograph, and the reproduction of Fred's old adobe where I spent many happy hours as a young man when helping to gather old renegade steers and unbranded wild cattle.

To Mrs. Marion Anderson I wish to say "thank you" for the reproduction of the photo furnished of some of many specimens of Indian pottery she gathered down through the years of the past.

To Louise Guanche, Adeline Elliott, Calistro Torte, and Pat Cassero, I wish to say "thank you" for the photos and other help they gave me as descendants of the Indians of Anza-Borrego Desert.

To Mr. and Mrs. Paul Cogley of Hemet, California, I cannot say enough to express my thanks for the fine job they did in reproducing photos, including old tintypes and other photos dating back as far as 1875.

To Mr. and Mrs. Eddie DuVall of Old-Borego Store, I wish to express appreciation for their having furnished me with a place to park my trailer-house where I could have electricity while refreshing my memory concerning places in the Anza-Borrego Desert after being absent from the area for about thirty years.

To Mrs. Edyth McGowan of Julian, I wish to express appreciation for the time she gave for tape recordings concerning her father, John McCain, who when he passed away in 1948, was about the last one of the old-timers who came to California with ox-teams.

Now last, but certainly not least, I am greatly indebted to Ann Elizabeth Wissler for the day she handed me the keys to her place on Mill Creek in the San Bernardino Mountains and informed me that she wanted me to go there to do my writing. In a corner of the front room, beside the fireplace with a fire built from wood furnished by Jim Wellman of the 101 Ranch in the San Jacinto Mountains, along with wood furnished by Ann, I have spent many hours of day and night struggling with punctuation, grammar, spelling, and that old portable Underwood typewriter. I feel that it would have been impossible for me to have found a more suitable place for my struggle.

CHAPTER 1

COMANCHE COUNTY TEXAS, TO CALIFORNIA IN 1864

IN THE EVENING of October 12, 1864, the families of John Taylor, John Ward, and Elliott Hicks arrived at Carrizo Creek within the boundaries of what is now known as the Anza-Borrego State Park situated in the southern part of California not so very far from the Mexican Border. Their ox-teams were weary, hungry and thirsty after lugging the heavy covered wagons over the stretch of Desert from Indian Well, a distance of about thirty-two miles.

In the latter part of February of this same year, John Taylor who was the husband of my father's sister, Margaret, had learned of a wagon-train scheduled to leave sometime in the spring from a point on the Concho River and the destination was to be California.

Taylor in his diary writes of having hurried off from his homestead in Comanche County, Texas, to buy oxen and wagon, with the highest of hopes to join the wagon-train. He had to travel into Williamson County, in central Texas, a distance of about one hundred twenty miles to find the necessary equipment for making the trip to California. To raise money for the buying of oxen and wagon, Taylor had sold part of his cattle, some hogs, and his one share in the school house in Comanche. His homestead, consisting of one hundred sixty acres, and about thirty head of cattle he left in charge of my grandfather (Asa Reed) to dispose of as best he could.

The Taylor Diary indicates that he was one of many deserters from the Southern Army at that time, for he wrote of having to do everything in secret, which made his procedures very difficult. The diary reads that Taylor started his journey to California April 15th, 1864, for he wrote:

"I set out on the evening of April 15th with a well written transfer from Major Erath of Concho County, there to report to the Captain of Militia in ten days. There were few who knew my intentions, it being reported that I was going to Concho to attend stock of cattle belonging to W. W. Chandler living on Pecan Bayou. I traveled on the 15th only about five miles to the Widow Liggins' where her son, Giles, joined me for the purpose of traveling with me as far as the Concho where he had a brother, both deserters."

April 16th the Taylor Party traveled 14 miles to a camp where they met a man by the name of Orright from whom they learned what they wished to know about the wagon-train they wished to join. Traveling with Taylor up to this time was his father-in-law (Asa Reed) and a man by the name of Arch Parker, who evidently were going along to help in getting on the way, and to know that he was successful in making contact with other members who were to make up the wagon-train to California. At this point, Taylor wrote in his diary of their cutting a bee-tree for the honey, which no doubt was part of a plan to live off the land wherever possible.

For the date of April 17th, Taylor in his diary again gives the impression that he was planning desertion from the Southern Army to leave with the wagon-train for California, for he again wrote of having to keep his intentions on the quiet:

"We traveled about 14 miles to the Pecan Bayou on the 17th. Mr. Chandler came to our camp tonight and expressed himself uneasy for fear the Military would deal harshly with him for helping me off. But I told him they would never know through me that I was going to do more than to attend to his cattle, and when they found out I was gone, to express himself as surprised that I had disappointed him about attending his cattle, and all would be well."

The following three days the Taylor Party traveled about forty-six miles. The first night they camped on a branch of the Areano, the second night at Home Creek, and at the end of the third day they were nearing the Colorado River that they intended to cross a little above the Concho. On April 21st they crossed the Colorado River of Texas, and went on to the Concho where they expected to find other wagons, but were disappointed when they found no wagons in camp. The following day after traveling up the Concho River about three miles they overtook the wagons with the occupants all intending to join the wagon-train. These wagons belonged to the Wards, Elliots, and McKees. From this point the wagons traveled together, covering a distance of about 18 miles to where they caught up with the wagons of other families and learned that they were having trouble because of a number of cases of whooping cough. The Taylors, Wards and Elliots camped before crossing the river to avoid coming in contact with those who were sick, but the McKees crossed on over to join relatives in the other camp.

At this point there were enough men in the train that they began to feel more secure concerning possible trouble with the Indians, a situation with which they had been faced since leaving Comanche. Fortunately, the Indians had not given any trouble, so their main hindrance had been bad roads over most of the way, and a great part of the time they were following only the tracks of other wagons traveling without a road to follow, and presumably all headed for the same point.

At the camp on the Concho, the wagons all stayed over until the 11th of May for the purpose of resting their teams, and to wait for other wagons that were known to be following up. Camping at this point gave the stock about eighteen days to rest on feed and water, and some of the men took advantage of the opportunity to hunt buffalo, and to catch fish from the river which greatly helped in their food supply.

While staying over at this camp, a detachment of Militia with a Captain by the name of Mosely, from Brown County, paid a visit, and went back to report favorably upon what members of the camp were doing.

When time came for breaking up camp, the wagons were divided into three trains. The first was known as Ball's Train, the first to arrive on the Concho, and consisting of ten wagons. The occupants of this train were of nine families; the Balls, Stevens, McKees, Fitskens, Charles Whitlows, Allen Whitlows, Fosemans, Paynes, and P. Liggins. In addition to members of the families were several independent young men. Another train was made up of six wagons known as Ward's Train: The John Ward family, Elliot Hicks family, John Taylor family, and five families with Green Ward. A third train, referred to as Hick's train, consisted of one large family and a sizeable company of deserters from Arkansas, headed by Captain Tinon, to whom members of the train had furnished provisions, and they in turn had agreed to escort the wagons across the Staked Plains. There were twenty-six men in this company, and in addition fifteen or twenty Texas Rangers that were to travel with them as far as the Pecos River.

The first day on the road after the wagons had been made up into the three trains, was the 11th day of May, and they traveled over a distance of about ten miles of good road to a place where they made camp and stayed over two days because of the death of a child in the Stevens family. May 14th the wagons traveled a distance of only eight miles up the south side of the main Concho River, and again had good roads. Here again the wagons spent another day because of the death of one of Allen Whitlow's children. This was the second child the Whitlows had buried since starting on their journey.

May 16th the wagons were again on their way, and still traveling along the south side of the Concho. This day they traveled about eighteen miles before stopping to camp, and here again they stayed over a day because of the death of a child in the Elliot family. At this camp Mr. Isiah Bays, a deserter from Price's division, joined the train. He had left his family in Bell County to stay while he was away on this trip, and he proved himself to be of great value as a guide, for he had traveled the route when on his way to California in 1861. In his diary, John Taylor refers to Bays as being a good man as well as being a valuable guide.

May 18th wagons traveled in a southwesterly direction and crossed two prongs of the Concho. After crossing the second time they traveled up the north side of this prong for a distance of about five miles to where they came to the Overland Mail Route and made camp for the night. The following two days about twenty miles had been covered over rough rocky roads.

May 21st a distance of about ten miles was traveled over rough road to the head of the Concho River. At this point there was one of the old stage stations and the remains of a soldier's camp. Before making camp the wagons were moved on about half a mile to what was said to be the last water in the area. By this time there were about one-hundred-fifty in the train, and in Taylor's Diary he again makes mention of deserters from many parts of the country. The last wagons to join with them were known as the San Saba Train and made up of six wagons and four families that had been overtaken on the way up the Concho River. They had been traveling independently, and had not known that the other trains were following up behind. The four families in this train were the Coles, Newtons, and two families by the name of Chilson. In addition to the members of the families were a number of young men.

About 4 p.m., May 22nd, the wagons were all started into the desert area after filling all water containers. They traveled all that night before stopping to rest the teams at a place thought to be about twenty-five miles from the starting point the evening before. They unhitched the teams for only about an hour and then started on again planning to shorten the distance all they could before stopping for a longer rest. A distance of about eight miles was made this time before making camp. After leaving this dry camp they had traveled about five miles when they stopped for the Foseman family to bury one of their children near an old station. At the end of this day, just before dark, it started to rain, and the lead wagons with which Taylor was traveling stopped, the occupants thinking they were going to experience a very heavy storm. The storm soon passed over, and when the other wagons came along they kept on traveling, so those who had turned loose their teams gathered them up and started on, soon to find plenty of water from the rain, and here the wagons were all stopped to make camp until the following morning.

May 24th the wagons all started slowly on their way, with all members of the train feeling joyful from having had the opportunity to get the stock so well watered where pools had been made by the rain that had fallen ahead of them. About noon of this day the wagons were all stopped for about three hours before starting on the last stretch of road through a canyon that would lead them to the Pecos River. Arriving at the Pecos they found the water to be very muddy and rather salty and the only wood available was the roots of trees which had to be dug from the ground. Evidently those who had traveled over the route before them had burned up all the wood above the ground. Grass was very scarce for the stock, but they stayed over a day to give the stock some much-needed rest, for the distance back to the Concho was about eighty miles.

About an hour before sundown the evening of May 26th, the wagon-trains left the camp on the Pecos River and traveled until about midnight when they stopped and put out a guard. Continuing on their way when morning came, they arrived at Antelope Spring about noon and found the water to be strong with soda, and wood was very scarce. At this camp, Captain Tinon, during trouble with one of his men, fired three shots, missing the man each time, but wounding a little boy of the train.

May 28th the wagon-train moved a distance of about ten miles to a place known as Camp Stockton where they found plenty of water and good grass for the stock. Finding feed and water conditions good at this point, they stayed over for four days to give the teams more rest, and to avoid traveling in the rain. The army camp here had been destroyed, and the Taylor diary reads that perhaps the destruction was the work of Glen Sibbly's men. In the diary John Taylor again writes of deserters, and records that about forty of them overtook the wagon-train at Fort Stockton, and that they were on their way to Mexico. At this camp the cavalry all left the wagon-train, some on their way to Mexico, and others going to El Paso with the intention of going to Missouri.

On June 2nd the wagons leaving Camp Stockton traveled a distance of about eight miles to Leon Hole, where they again found soda water, no wood, and the weather was very rainy. June 3rd, after traveling over a distance of about sixteen miles, they made camp on the prairie where wood, water, and grass conditions were very poor. June 4th, the wagons arrived at an old stage station after traveling over rocky hill roads and along a creek bed.

The following day they traveled into a mountainous country where they found plenty of water, good grass and a fair supply of wood, so they stayed over two days while it rained. The mountains nearby were covered by fine timber, but there was not much along the road.

Leaving this camping place the morning of June 8th, the wagon-train covered a distance of about ten miles, first over a rocky hill, then along a winding creek through the mountains, and after crossing the creek about twenty times they made camp for the night.

June 9th the wagon-train arrived at the old Fort Davis, after traveling a distance of about nine miles. About one half mile from the old fort they found a grove of beautiful cottonwoods where they established camp with water, grass and wood all being plentiful. In the diary John Taylor wrote of visiting the fort and finding it in horrible ruin, but in a beautiful location. He describes everything that would burn as being in ashes, and of course, everything that was metal telling a story of ruin. Taylor wrote of this ruin being the work of General Sibbly.

June 10th the wagons moved on from Fort Davis passing a station known as Barrel Springs, the spring being about three hundred yards from the station. At this place the water was not too plentiful, no wood, so before making camp they traveled on for about two miles to where they had grass for the stock. June 12, they arrived at Dead Man's Hole described as having the best water on the entire route. Grass and wood being plentiful, the teams were rested for two days before going on to Horn's Well where the water situation was found to be very poor, due to the fact that the well had been very well filled up.

On June 17th traveling on to Eagle Springs they again found a poor water condition, so they went back about four miles to where they had good grass and water was plentiful. Even though the water was described as being plentiful at this camp, they had to dig into the sand to better water the stock. Knowing the next water would be at the Rio Grande, about forty miles distant, they stayed over a day at this camp.

The ox-teams and wagons were on the way again late in the evening of June 19th with some of the horsemen riding on ahead of the teams and the heavy wagons. They traveled until nearly daylight before stopping about two hours to rest the animals. On these long stretches of travel between water, they had to keep moving as much as possible to avoid the stock being too thirsty when they again had the opportunity to drink, so after the two-hour rest they were on the way again not too long after sunrise. This morning they traveled until about 10 a.m. over a stretch of good road which was a great relief to the animals pulling the heavy loads. That evening they were on the way again entering a canyon through which they had to travel over some of the roughest road on the entire trip. The distance over which they had to travel this rough road was about twelve miles to the Rio Grande River where they arrived about one hour before day.

Upon arrival at the Rio Grande they received word that about fifteen Federal soldiers were camped near by, and this was good news to them because they were still traveling in country not too safe from raids by renegade white men or from the Indians. The following day was June 21st, and while staying over for the day the soldiers came to visit them and informed they intended to escort the wagon-train for the next sixty-five miles. The soldiers were on their way to the main camp, right on the route the wagons were to travel. While camping on the Rio Grande at this place, some of the men swam over to the Mexican side of the river.

On June 22nd the wagon-train traveled only about five miles and made camp at Fort Quitman, another fort that had been thoroughly destroyed. At this camp the commander of the soldiers asked that the different divisions of the train travel more closely together, with Ward's Train, the one with which John Taylor's family had been traveling, to remain in the lead as before. The following four days the wagons covered a distance of about fifty-two miles along the Rio Grande, camping at times on sloughs extending out from the river, and each night they had plenty of water and good grass, the water being somewhat brackish and rather muddy. On the 25th they passed the first house seen since leaving Home Creek, not long after leaving Comanche. The house was occupied by Mexicans.

June 27th they traveled a distance of seven miles and made camp at San Lasan where they saw the U.S. flag waving in the breeze. The Taylor Diary records that this was the first time he had seen the Stars and Stripes since before the war started, and he wrote that the feeling it gave him could better be imagined than described. Taylor also wrote that once more under the Stars and Stripes he felt he had been relieved from bondage, that he once again felt at home. Camp was set up about two miles from town where grass was very scarce, and that night some of the oxen strayed into an unfenced corn field belonging to the Mexicans and caused a ten dollar damage bill being paid by members of the train.

While staying over June 28th, members of the train visited the town and bought vegetables which served them well in helping to cure many cases of scurvy. After leaving San Lasan the morning of June 29th, the wagons were moved over a distance of seven miles of good road and camp for the night was where they had good grass, not long after passing another small town. By this time the animals pulling the wagons were getting weary and thin, so they stopped whenever they found good grass, not being concerned about distances traveled.

July 1st the wagons arrived at Fort Bliss to make camp after traveling about ten miles over good road, though muddy from recent rains. Fort Bliss was in ruins as had been Fort Davis and Fort Quitman. This camping place being near to town, grass and wood were very scarce. Straw was purchased to feed the stock, and while here they learned they were among thieves when a horse was stolen from a young man traveling with the wagon-train.

July 2nd the train moved about eight miles before making camp at a place where grass again was very scarce. This day they drove into a place referred to as Franklin where the California Regiment was stationed. As the wagons arrived in town the brass band was playing and the soldiers were marching. At this place, the members of the train all took the oath of allegiance to the flag, and received passports to take them through to California. After drawing rations for about twenty days, the wagons were moved on for a distance of about six miles before making camp near the river, and again they found a very poor grass situation. The following day they traveled nine miles to a place near Camp Grant where they found good grass, to they stayed over three days to recuperate the stock.

July 7th, after traveling about seven miles, the train arrived at Cottonwood where they again found good grass, but water was rather bad. Being a bit careless at this camping place where they spent seventeen days to further recuperate the teams, a number of their stock were stolen. Taylor recorded in his diary that he was fortunate enough not to suffer any losses to the thieves. However, he sold one horse while there and states that he had only one horse left to be stolen. John Taylor and his children had been sick while at this camp.

July 24th the wagon-train was on the way again, and after traveling eight miles they camped near the river where they found the grass very good. The following three days the wagons were moved over a distance of about eighteen miles, the first night camping about two miles outside Las Cruces. At this point in the Taylor Diary, I do not find any mention of El Paso, but mention of Las Cruces would indicate they were in what is now New Mexico. At this camp there was very little grass, no wood, but plenty of water from the recent rains. The 26th the wagons were not moved but instead the stock were rested while members of the train were busy buying supplies for about sixty days and getting ready to cross the river. The 27th the wagons were moved only about three miles to the ferry where they found wood and water, but very little grass.

Very little progress was made the 28th because of having to cross the river. The crossing was made about one half mile above Mesilla, a town described as being a beautiful place. Another reason for the delay was due to the death of a child in the Neighbors family caused from a fall out of the wagon. In the diary Taylor describes the Mesilla Valley as being one of very fertile soil and growing many fields of wheat and corn. Timber was very scarce in this area, and the fields were farmed mostly by Mexicans, with the fields not being fenced so the stock had to be closely guarded.

After traveling about three miles July 29th the wagons were moved past a town by the name of La Cache. At this point they left the valley, traveling across the plains in a westerly direction. About eight miles after passing the town, they made camp for the night where there was no wood or water, but good grass. When morning came Taylor's only horse, one belonging to the Wards, and one belonging to the Sims family had been stolen by the Mexicans. Some of the men trailed the stolen horses back to La Cache, but there they could no longer follow the trail.

July 30th and 31st very good time was made, covering a distance of about thirty miles. They now had good roads, but where they camped the first night they found very little grass, poor water conditions, but for this night the wood supply was plentiful. The second night they camped at a tank where water and wood were scarce, but the stock had good grass.

This day was the beginning of the month of August, and through the 1st and 2nd about sixteen miles of progress had been made. The first night they camped on the prairie where there was no water, but wood and grass in good supply. The second night their camp was at Cook Springs where the stock had plenty of grass and water, but wood for the camp fires was difficult to find. August 3rd, the wagons had to travel through Cook's Canyon for about three miles over bad road. After passing through the Canyon they again had good road for about eight miles to where they camped without wood or water, but grass was good.

August 4th, after traveling about seven miles, they arrived at Nimbres River or Creek, and at this place they found plenty of water, good grass, but again wood was difficult to find. After stopping here, members of the train were pleased to learn that soldiers were camped near by. Grass and water being plentiful at this camping place, no traveling was done the following four days for the stock were in need of food and rest. A man by the name of William Cole was buried at this camping place, and John Taylor in the diary referred to him as being an old man.

August 9th the wagons were on their way again, and traveled through the 15th arriving at water where grass was plentiful, but was another one of the many places where wood was scarce. At this point the wagons split up, with the Liggins, Payne and Foseman families of the original train going with the San Sabe Train that had joined along the route. During this seven days of travel the wagon-train covered a distance of about ninety miles, passing Cow Springs, Soldier's Farewell, Barney's Station, and Stream Peak. At no camping place since

August 9th had wood, water and grass, all three, been plentiful. Sometimes finding a place where the stock could be watered, but, there was no grass, the stock would be watered, then the wagons would be moved on to where the stock could have grass. Some strips of the road had been good, but much of the time very rough and rocky.

The evening of August 16th they made camp for the night where there was good grass, but no wood or water. The road being good this day they traveled a distance of about fifteen miles. On August 17th, the wagon-train now moving through Arizona, arrived at Apache Pass after traveling over some more bad road. They made camp at Soldier's Station where for a change wood, water, and grass were all plentiful.

From the morning of August 18th through the 26th, the wagon-train moved on one hundred and four miles, arriving near Tucson, Arizona, described in the Taylor diary as being a Mexican town. The first night on this stretch of road, they camped on the prairie where there was good grass, but no wood or water. The night of August 19th they camped at Sulphur Springs, the following night at San Pedro where soldiers were stationed, and once more water, wood and grass were all plentiful. So often along the entire route since leaving Comanche County, Texas, the three necessities for the making of a good camp were not all present at the same time. The night of August 23rd, after having three days of rough road, the camping place was Seneca Creek, where they stayed over the following day to take advantage of having good grass, water and wood plentiful, making another good place to rest and recuperate the teams. On their way again the 25th, they had a dry camp that night with no wood and very little grass. From there they traveled to the camp near Tucson.

August 27th they again stayed over to take advantage of good grass and water for the stock. Moving again the 28th through the 31st, the wagons arrived at Blue Water Well, referred to as being deep. The night of the 28th they camped at a water hole where the water supply was very poor, but grass and wood were plentiful. The 29th they covered nine miles of sandy road and camped at a station well where they could water the stock but had no wood and grass was scarce. The night of the 30th after going about ten miles, they made a dry camp where wood and grass were plentiful. The 31st they traveled about fifteen miles to arrive at Blue Water Well.

September 1st, after about eighteen miles of journey, they camped at another well referred to as a deep one where they could water the stock but the grass was scarce. The 2nd the wagon-train traveled a distance of sixteen miles over good road and made a dry camp where wood and grass was scarce.

The 3rd of September, after going about nine miles, the wagons arrived at a station called Sacaton situated on the Gila River. This place was one of the outer settlements of the Pima Indians, a tribe that had been there for years and governed by an agent of the U.S. Government. These Indians are referred to in the diary as being a friendly people to the white man, but along with another tribe farther down the river known as the Maricopas, were at war with the Apaches. The Pimas at that time were raising wheat along with other types of farming, and some of them came into camp and sold pumpkins and watermelons to members of the wagon-train. The fresh pumpkins and watermelons served as a real treat after so long a time on the road. Being a good place to camp, the teams were given a day's rest.

September 5th the wagons were moved on again for about twelve miles over good road to White's Mill where they found Mr. White to be an agent for the Indians and a very accommodating man. Water was plentiful there, but the same old story of wood and grass being scarce. The following day after again having about twelve miles of good road, they camped at Maricopa Wells where they were fortunate enough to find water and grass plentiful. This being a good place to recuperate the teams, they spent eight days before starting on again.

While camping at Maricopa Wells, the members of the wagon-train were informed there was very little grass along the way to Fort Yuma on the Colorado River. After wondering for quite some time just what to do, the owners of most of the wagons decided to take the route toward Prescott which they had been told was about one hundred miles farther than the route to Yuma, but good grass would be found in the more mountainous area.

After the owners of most of the wagons decided to take the route toward Prescott, John Ward, with whom the Taylor family had been traveling since arriving on the Concho River in Texas, spoke up and said if one other wagon would join him, he would take the route to Yuma. Taylor said that he would, and then Mr. Hicks joined with them in the idea, and they decided to start the following day.

The morning of September 15th the three families: the Wards, the Hicks, and the Taylors were started on their way to get to the Colorado River at Fort Yuma, and after traveling about twelve miles they made camp for the night at a tank where rain water had collected, but wood and grass were very scarce. The 16th the wagons remained at the tank until evening before starting on the thirty mile trip to the Gila Bend Station on the Gila River. The wagons were kept moving all night, and arrived at Gila Bend the 17th where the water supply was very good, but, as they had been informed at Maricopa, the wood and grass supply was very poor.

Leaving Gila Bend on September 18th, the wagons of the three familes were on the road to the Colorado River for seventeen days before arriving there. Along the way grass had been scarce as was expected, but most of the time wood and water were plentiful. The distance over which the wagons had to travel from Gila Bend to Yuma was about one hundred and thirty-five miles, the route over which the wagon road wound its way in those day, so for the time they traveled they averaged less than ten miles per day.

On the trek from Gila Bend to Yuma, they camped four times on the Gila River. Two of their camps had been at stations for which no name was given in the diary, one night at Oatman Flats, and a night at Burk's Station. On September 22nd the ox teams were rested near a ranch where members of the train bought beef and vegetables which made a pleasing change of diet. On their way again the 23rd, they found a place off the road, where, for a change, they had all three of the necessities for the making of a good place to camp. This day the oxen had to lug the wagons over twelve miles of sandy road.

The night of September 24th the wagons had passed Texas Hill, and the place where they camped was at the point of a hill on the Gila River. The 25th the wagons passed Mohawk, and about seven miles farther down the road at Laguna, they stopped to camp for the night where the stock fared well, and there was a plentiful supply of wood for the fires. The 27th they stayed over for a day near Antelope Peak.

On the 28th the wagons were on the way again, and after having about fifteen miles of sandy road they arrived at Mission Camp to stay for the night. The following three days on the way to the Colorado, they did not travel very far either day, for grass and water were plentiful, and the stock were given the advantage of the situation for recuperation while they had the opportunity.

After crossing over the Colorado River the 4th of October, the three families spent the rest of the day in Fort Yuma where they bought supplies to last for thirty days, as this would be the last place they could get such supplies until they arrived in the Warner Ranch or Temecula areas. In Taylor's Diary he wrote concerning their arrival at Fort Yuma:

"Fort Yuma is a beautiful fort situated on the California side of the river. I can now say for the first time that I am in California. Our spirits were greatly revived when we got here and found three steamboats landing to receive and take off freight. There is also a little town on the east side of the river called Arizona City. We had no grass here for our teams. This place presents rather a business-like appearance. It is a kind of Government place for landing supplies for the District of Arizona. We here set in on a desert of one hundred miles where there is nothing but mesquite beans for our teams to eat."

The morning of October 5th the families of Ward, Taylor, and Hicks left Fort Yuma taking the left hand road that would for a time lead them across and below the Mexican Border in order to detour to the south of the sand dunes through which runs Highway 80 between Holtville and Yuma. (After the development of Imperial Valley was well under way, the old Plank Road was laid across the sand dunes, and parts of the old planks can still be seen when traveling through the dunes on Highway 80. I can remember hearing the Old Plank Road mentioned in the conversation of persons owning automobiles in the early days of Imperial Valley.)

The day the covered wagons left Fort Yuma they were moved over about twenty-five miles of rather bad road before finding a place where the teams would have good grass and could be rested for a day. On their way again the 7th of October, the ox teams had the advantage of about eight miles of good road before arriving at Cook's Well where the teams were rested until night. That night after traveling seven more miles, the wagons arrived at Seven Wells. This last seven miles had been over sandy roads but they were rewarded by having mesquite beans and water. On October 8th the wagons were not started on the way until late evening, and then they were kept moving most of the night before stopping for a dry camp, where there were mesquite beans for the stock and wood for the camp. The 9th they arrived at Alamo Well where the stock again had mesquite beans and water. On the 10th the wagons were again started late in the evening and traveled over sandy road most of the night. At this stop the teams were watered at Indian Well, then the wagons were on the way again, starting over the thirty-two-mile stretch of dry desert to Carrizo Creek, and to make this stretch of desert to the best of advantage for the stock, it was necessary to travel continuously until arrival at the Carrizo Creek water.

Following the date of October 12th in John Taylor's Diary, he wrote:

"Got to Carrizo Creek in the evening. No grass or mesquite beans. Water. Here two yoke of oxen of Ward's ran away and went right back on the desert. There was no horse in the train able to follow the oxen any great distance, so I being the most able to walk, started to follow the runaways, taking along a little pony of Ward's. This was about nine o'clock the morning of October 13th, and after about six miles I decided I could make better time on foot, so I tied the pony to an old dagger stalk and took out on foot to follow the trail of the oxen, thinking of course, that I would soon be back with them. I walked as fast as I could until night, and no oxen yet. The trail of the oxen missed the Indian Well about twelve miles and I thought I was near the road all the way. About an hour after night I thought I heard the bell. I was still trailing by moonlight, and rushed on as fast as I could, though I was very tired. In about two hours I came in sight of them. They took fright and ran off nearly out of hearing. I had brought nothing to eat with me but two biscuits. The weather being very warm, my canteen of water did not last very long. I still rushed on for four or five miles farther until I got near the oxen again. They took another fright as before, and ran off in a long trot as far as I could hear the bell. Well, I could not strike a trot myself to save my life, so I sat down to rest and study what to do. I now began to realize my situation. Something over forty miles from camp, on a hot sandy desert without food or water. A place where a number of men had been lost and died from thirst. It was now about midnight when I started back very tired and hungry. I was very dry for water, though I considered my chances of getting back very good if no sand storm spoiled the road, but I traveled about twelve miles before I struck it."

"I came to the road at Indian Well, where I drank as much water as I wanted and laid down and rested for about an hour. I then filled my canteen and started back two hours before the sun in the morning. It was about thirty-two miles distant to the camp. I could not travel more than about a mile and a half so I stopped and rested for about an hour. My water did not last longer than about twelve o'clock, so that night I was very thirsty again, but still I hobbled along, and about midnight when I got to where I tied the pony it was still there. The pony had been there all this time without food or water. Here I quenched my thirst with the bottle of water I had left on my saddle, and I thought it the best drink of water I ever had."

"I saddled my pony and started, but found the pony could not travel any faster than I, though it was a little easier on me as I was given out entirely. Well, about three hours longer brought me to where I had left the wagons, but they had gone on, so I traveled about four miles farther and came to where they were breaking camp. They were all overjoyed to see me, as they thought I had been lost on the desert, and were going to go back and hunt for me. This experience satisfied me that an ox can travel many miles without water when traveling of his own free will."

The date was now October 15th and Taylor being very tired, sleepy and hungry, decided to stay at this second camp on Carrizo Creek while his family and the Wards went on to Caliente where the Hicks family had gone to camp and rest. At Caliente the stock could get water and some grass, so the three families stayed for two days to rest the stock and to do the family washings.

October 18th the wagons were moved to Vallecito over the very sandy strip of road between the two places. At Vallecito the water and grass situation was good enough that they stayed over for four days to further recuperate the stock. In the diary John Taylor did not mention of himself during the time they stayed at Caliente and Vallecito, but it is most likely that he enjoyed the resting periods at these two camps as much as did the oxen, and there can be no doubt the little pony that had been tied to the dagger for so many hours without food or water enjoyed his share of recuperation. I know of very few men today who would have the courage and stamina to put out the effort John Taylor did to bring back the runaway oxen. Such an effort required the degree of determination possessed by the old-timers through necessity.

When the time came to be traveling on their way from Valle-cito, Taylor wrote of having about eight miles of very hilly rocky road to cover, including a bad canyon to go through. This strip of road, of course, was first up over the Mason Hill where the road was very steep, with sharp turns, and then out of the Mason Valley into Box Canyon of about one and one half miles in length. History tells us that the road through Box Canyon was first blazed with hand tools used by the Mormon Battalion under command of Lieutenant Colonel Philip St. George Cooke. At a place about half way through the canyon there is a rock bluff high enough to cause the building of a narrow road along the side of the hill which is the east wall of the canyon. Fortunately, this bluff in the bottom of the canyon is situated where the canyon walls are not so very high or steep, so the problem of building a road around was not as difficult as would have been in other places along the canyon. History tells us that the Mormon Battalion blazed their way through the canyon in January of 1847, and in the latter part of the year 1858 the first Butterfield Stage Coach passed through Box Canyon.

After passing through Box Canyon into Blair Valley, the ox teams were relieved for a time from having to lug the wagons through sand and over rough roads. Where the old road left Blair Valley, the oxen had a strenuous struggle in pulling the wagons over a very steep hill for about fifty yards. When walking over this short strip of very steep road now, I think of my father telling about the patience of the ox if he was given plenty of time where the going was rough, and he said that he never felt he was stuck as long as the patient oxen could move a wagon as much as only six inches at a time. This very steep climb in the old Butterfield route is about one half mile to the east of where the surfaced road passes out of Blair Valley when traveling toward the north.

After pulling the wagons over the very steep hill coming out of Blair Valley, the oxen had very good road most of the way to the water at the lower end of San Felipe Valley. At this camp a man with a team of two horses and a wagon met the covered wagons. The team of horses and the wagon had been sent to the Wards by a man by the name of Greenwade because of the loss of his oxen at Carrizo. Somehow, word of the straying oxen had gotten ahead of them.

In the diary Taylor records that after traveling about eight miles from the camp at the lower end of San Felipe Valley, they passed a Mexican village, so this perhaps was where some old adobe buildings were still standing when I was on my first cattle drive to Imperial Valley in 1910.

As the weary oxen teams passed from the San Felipe Valley after the many weeks in arid desert land, they were getting into an entirely different type of country, and were nearing their destination not too far from San Bernardino, California. On October 25th they passed through Warner Ranch and arrived at Temecula the following day, where the families bought hay for their teams, and food for themselves.

The Taylor family settled in the vicinity of San Bernardino and later John Taylor was successful in campaigning for and being elected public administrator in the City of San Bernardino. I remember hearing my father tell how, during the campaign, persons would be heard saying they were going to vote for the little man who drove the bull-team from Texas.

Near April 1, 1867, my grandfather and grandmother (Asa and Naoma Reed) arrived at Vallecito with covered wagons and ox teams, along with a small herd of cattle that they had brought from Comanche County, Texas, and they had traveled all the way over the same route as had the Taylors. John Hart had been buried on a little hill a very short distance to the east of the Vallecito Stage Station, just about two weeks before the arrival of the Reeds and other members of the wagon-train. I remember hearing my father speak of the Widow Hart being at the Vallecito Station.

Members of the Reed family traveling from Texas to California with ox teams in 1867 included the parents (Asa and Naoma) ; three sons: William, John, and Quitman; and two daughters; Mrs. Frances Parks, and Mrs. Martha Robinson. I started out with the idea of giving a brief mention of the descendants of the old-timers of which I am writing, but I found that it would sum up to a task beyond the time that I have. Even with the help of my father's (Quitman Reed) brothers and sisters, I found that it would be a task too much

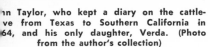

[...]n Taylor, who kept a diary on the cattle-[dri]ve from Texas to Southern California in [18]64, and his only daughter, Verda. (Photo from the author's collection)

Asa Reed and his wife, Naoma, arrived at Vallecito with covered wagons and ox teams in 1867, after more than five months on the trail. (Photo taken in 1875, from the Quitman Reed collection)

for me as far past twenty-one as I am. However, I do know that William Reed never had a family; the sons and daughters of Mrs. Frances Parks have all passed away; there are two daughters and a son of John Reed still living; the Robinsons moved back to Texas, and I lost all trace of them. I am the only one left of the Quitman Reed family. I do mention Vina Reed, the eldest daughter of John Reed, in my acknowledgements, as being the one who furnished me with the Taylor Diary.

A short time ago, a grand-daughter of Mrs. Frances Parks (Mrs. Ruby Brubaker) asked me what brought the Reed and Parks families from Texas to California, and I told her it was the search for gold and cattle range.

The Reed and Parks families, after arrival in Southern California, first settled near Los Angeles, but after hearing the soldiers tell of meadows in the mountains northeast of Temecula where they cut hay with the old hand scythes for the cavalry animals, they decided to take a look at the area. Asa Reed being a surveyor, they learned that there was a sizeable piece of meadow outside the Cahuilla Indian Reservation on the west end, so they settled there. After a time, William and Quitman moved to some meadows to the northwest of Cahuilla that still bear the name of Reed Valley. When arriving there they learned there were a few grizzly bears in the area, and they trapped two right near to where my father built his homestead house where I spent the first two years of my life. The graves of Asa and Naoma Reed are on a little hill right near where this old house stood. The Cahuilla and Reed Valley is where my father started in the cattle business with cows driven from Comanche County, Texas, to Southern California. A few days ago, I took a horn from one of the old lead steers they drove from Texas, and left it at the San Jacinto Museum. Along with the horn I took the branding irons of William and Quitman Reed. As I stated before, I must not try to go into family histories, but I do want to make mention of the night the Reed and Parks families stayed at Temecula when they first arrived in Southern California.

Their camp in the vicinity of Temecula was on the old Wolf Place where the Pauba Ranch headquarters are at this time, and living there at the time was the Charlie Thomas family who later moved into the San Jacinto Mountains in what is now known as the Garner Ranch. A daughter, Victoria, was born that night to the Thomas family, and my grandmother (Naoma Reed) assisted in bringing her into the world.

About six years later, after the Thomases moved into the San Jacinto Mountains, my father when hauling freight with the ox teams for Charlie, ran over little "Vicky" as everyone called her. He ran over her with the hind wheel of the empty ox wagon when the whip fell from the seat and the little girl dashed into the way of the wagon to get the whip. Of course, everyone was badly frightened, but she was not injured to any great degree. A doctor stated that a grown person perhaps would have suffered more injury than did the little child. I went to visit with "Vicky" when she was at the age of 91, and the incident of being run over with the ox wagon was the first thing she talked about. I am not sure, but at this writing, January 1, 1963, I believe that Mrs. Victoria Brooks is still alive and living in Hemet, California. If so, she is one of the very few of the old-timers left.

CHAPTER 2

DESERT CATTLE DRIVE OF 1886

ONE MORNING somewhere near March 1, 1886, about two thousand steers were being rested at the water in Carrizo Creek of the Anza-Borrego Desert. Most of these cattle were lying down to get some much-needed rest after having traveled over many miles of long dry distances between places where that many cattle could be watered. This herd of steers had been started on the drive from the great Empire Ranch, owned and operated by Walter Vail, about forty miles southeast of Tucson, Arizona.

The major reason that this cattle drive had been undertaken was because of prohibitive freight rates being charged by the railroad companies, and the destination was the Warner Ranch in San Diego County, California, where Mr. Vail had extensive cattle operations. The Trail Boss of this cattle drive was a young Texan by the name of Tom Turner who felt confident that with the help of cowboys working on the Empire Ranch he could successfully move the herd across the long stretches of hazardous desert to the ranch in California, so after discussing the idea thoroughly with Walter Vail, preparations for the drive were soon in the making. A chuckwagon to be drawn by mules or horses had to be equipped with the necessary grubboxes, food supplies sufficient to last for quite some time, dutch-ovens, and other cooking utensils, and the most important of all, the water containers for the necessary supply for cooking and for drinking water for the cowboys over the long stretches of desert.

To successfully make such a drive with so many cattle, the Trail Boss must be a man of integrity, loyalty, unlimited courage, determination, and have the ability to maintain the respect and loyalty of the men working under him. He had to be a man who at all times would take upon himself his share of whatever hardships they experienced. The old-time cowboys on such cattle drives had to endure many long, sleepless and thirsty hours, and there could not always be any great degree of regularity in getting their meals. Their horses had to endure the hardship of many thirsty hours, as did the cattle they were driving. However, I don't believe there ever have been men working as a group, who apparently enjoyed their work—despite hardships—as did the old-time cowboys.

The old-time cowboy was considered by some as a rough type of person, but the majority possessed a code of honor by which they lived, and there were many of them who were willing to go to their death in defense of what they believed to be their honor. When they gave their word they kept it, and in living up to what they believed to be their code of honor they saw much more of death, but much less of vice than do we living at the present time. Many of these men no doubt looked upon death as a thing much cleaner than vice, and because of living so close to nature they were without chance to master the outward graces that have so often been mistaken for the marks of a gentleman.

Young Tom Turner was a man of enough experience in the cattle world to know that on such long treks cattle must be "moved" slowly, rather than to be "driven" at the fast rate of speed we so often see in western television programs. The cowboys helping on this cattle drive were Mexicans—vaqueros—with the exception of Ed Vail (a brother to Walter), Tom Turner, and two young fellows who had joined the cattle drive near Yuma. These two young white boys were traveling with several head of horses and when they offered their services to help with the cattle rather than to cross the desert alone, Turner accepted their offer and the two young men introduced themselves as brothers by the name of Fox, and along the way they proved themselves as willing and likable fellows.

From the Empire Ranch to Yuma, feed and water conditions had been fairly good, so about a month's time had been spent between these two points. Turner knew the advantage to be gained by taking plenty of time wherever water and grass would permit, so that the cattle would be in the best condition possible when leaving the Colorado River to travel over the long stretches of sandy desert that lay ahead of them.

After arriving at Yuma, and while resting the cattle, scouting trips were made down the river to the south in search of a place most suitable for the crossing of the herd. A place in the river near what was then known as Willow Lake was chosen for the crossing, for there the river was rather wide, more shallow, the water not running so swiftly, and the banks not so steep.

To successfully move two thousand steers over the desert between the Colorado River and Carrizo Creek was quite a responsibility. No one knew the exact location of any of the watering places, so this hampered them to considerable degree. Turner knowing the cattle must not be hurried, planned to keep the cattle moving at a reasonable pace as steadily as possible with an occasional short period of rest to maintain their stamina.

Before leaving the river every container on the chuck-wagon that would hold water was filled, for sound reasoning told them that if possible they must be prepared for the worst. The supply they could haul would have to serve for cooking and drinking water for the cowboys. The route of travel that lay ahead was the Butterfield Stage Route which dipped into Mexico in order to detour around the sand dunes through which Highway 80 now passes between Yuma, Arizona, and Holtville, California.

After moving the herd most of the time for two days and a night, the water supply on the chuck-wagon was running very low, and only one place had been found where the saddle horses could be watered. Tom Turner was riding point when a lead steer raised his head to sniff the air. The steer bawled lowly—as thirsty cattle will—and then quickened his pace in the direction from which the breeze was blowing. Turner knew the steer had smelled water, so let him lead the way, for experience had taught him that the steer would be a better guide than he, and his major hope was that there would be plenty of water for the thirsty cattle, the very weary men and horses, and the containers on the chuck-wagon could again be filled. Over a distance of about two miles the steer led the thirsty herd to a lake of fine clear water, and there can be no doubt, but what this lake of water was one of the most pleasing scenes ever experienced in the lives of the cowboys who had remained so cheerful and loyal through the hardships of the long distances and hours between watering places.

Even to this day, there are times and places where we who work with cattle must completely ignore the idea of an eight-hour day, and realize the importance of being loyal to a considerate boss, and to the owner of the cattle that have been entrusted to our care.

The cattle were held over at the lake of water for several days, in order for men, horses and cattle to recuperate before starting on the way again. When time came that the herd was being moved after a good rest at the lake, not so many miles had been traveled when the lead steer again indicated that he smelled water, and led the way to it. Finding this other lake of water was of great help to the stock, for it lessened the miles of dry trek to Carrizo Creek.

After arrival at Carrizo Creek, the herd was held near the water to give men, horses, and the cattle a chance for more recuperation. The morning following the arrival at the Carrizo water, a two-horse carriage in which four men were riding came near where the chuckwagon was, and one of the men beckoned to Ed Vail, so he walked over to where the carriage was stopped to learn what the men wanted. When the spokesman asked if two young men who had several head of horses were traveling with the herd, Vail recognized him as being a sheriff from Arizona. One of the other men was then introduced as the sheriff's deputy, a third man, if I remember correctly, the one who was driving the team, was introduced as a California deputy, and the fourth as a rancher in Arizona from whom some horses had been stolen.

Evidently, the Arizona sheriff had learned the two young men with the horses were traveling with the Vail cattle, and he had trailed the herd to the Mexican Border, where he could no longer legally follow in pursuit of the young men whom he thought to possess the stolen horses. The sheriff, his deputy, and the owner of the horses that had been stolen, then took the train to Temecula where the fourth man had joined them in making the trip to Carrizo Creek with the team of horses and the carriage.

Mr. Vail then cautioned the sheriff and his men to be very careful for he knew the Fox brothers were well armed and very fast with their guns. The sheriff suggested the cowboys be told they were mining men who had come into the area to look at a mine near by. One of the Fox brothers asked Ed Vail who the strangers were and as the sheriff had suggested, he was told that the four men were there to look at a mine nearby, but for quite some time the strangers were eyed with suspicion.

The sheriff and his men were asked to eat at the chuckwagon, and all during the meal they talked about the mine they had come to see, so as time passed, the Fox brothers became more relaxed, and seemed to lose their suspicion. Soon after the men had finished their meal, the youngest of the Fox boys was standing by one of the front wheels of the wagon, and the other was leaning against the tailboard. Simultaneously, each of the Fox Boys was attacked by two men of the sheriff's party and disarmed.

The sheriff and one of his men had disarmed the elder one of the boys and managed to hold him, but the younger one, after being disarmed, jerked away from his attackers and started running up a wash with a deputy in close pursuit. After pursuing the young man for about one hundred yards, the deputy suddenly raised his gun and fired, which of course resulted in the young disarmed cowboy being shot from behind and dropping him in his tracks.

By this time the sheriff and his assistant had the handcuffs on the brother, and when Ed Vail looked up from where the body of the dead boy lay, he saw the handcuffed boy coming toward the fallen body of his brother. The officers told the handcuffed boy to stop, but he told them to go ahead and shoot him, for he intended to go to his dead brother. After standing and looking down at the body of of his dead brother for awhile, the handcuffed boy turned to Ed Vail and asked him to see that his brother's body was buried. Ed Vail assured the young man who had been so loyal and cheerful through

Virgie, the little mule used by the author to retrace many of the old trails in the Anza and Borrego areas. Virgie was killed when hit by a motor vehicle on Highway 38, in 1963.

Grave of Joe Fox, killed by a deputy sheriff at Carrizo Creek about March 1, 1886, when accused of horse theft in Arizona. (Photo taken by the author in 1930)

the hardships of the hazardous trek across the desert, that he could depend on the body being taken care of in the best manner possible under the existing situation.

The sheriff and his men left the body of the young man where he had fallen, and started on their way back to Temecula, taking the brother as their prisoner. Some of the cowboys dug a grave where the body of the Fox boy lay, and after wrapping him in his blanket, he was placed in the grave, covered with dirt, and then stones were used to cover the grave full length.

Perhaps the killing of this young unarmed man who had been so willing and cheerful during the hardships of the cattle drive from Yuma, was the major reason the herd was again on its way the following morning, and the men with the cattle were more than pleased to be getting away from the scene of such a tragedy.

The herd was on the road only a few more days in traveling from Carrizo to the Warner Ranch, and it requires only a small degree of imagination to realize the joy experienced by Ed Vail, Tom Turner, and all of the other men (including the cook) who had so faithfully done their part in making the cattle drive a success for the owner.

White men had not yet driven the Indians away from their adobe homes at the hot springs on Warner Ranch, so the cowboys who had missed so many baths while on the trip from Arizona, enjoyed bathing in the hot water, washing their clothes, and visiting and laughing with the Indians who could speak Spanish. The cowboys were then taken to Los Angeles where they saw the largest town they had ever been in, but only a short time passed before their feet were tired and sore from the sidewalks, and they were anxious to get back to the Empire Ranch, in Arizona, where they felt much more at home on horseback.

Soon after the return of the cowboys to the Empire Ranch, a meeting of cattlemen was called at what was then known as the Palace Hotel in Tucson, the purpose of the meeting being to discuss the establishment of a safe cattle trail from Tucson to the pasture lands in Southern California. From the experiences of the Vail Cattle Drive, Ed Vail was in a position to suggest the improvement of watering places at the old Butterfield Stage Stations along the way across the Colorado Desert (Anza-Borrego Desert), and to propose the building of a flat boat upon which cattle could be taken across the Colorado River.

When officials of the railroad company heard of the proposed meeting of cattlemen, they asked permission to have their representative present. Permission was granted, and soon after the meeting, an official letter was received stating that if no more cattle drives were made, the old freight rate on stock cattle would be restored.

For a good many years after the controversy over freight rates was settled, the Vails shipped cattle from the Empire Ranch to Beaumont, California, where they would be unloaded and driven over the old narrow dirt road through Lamb Canyon into the Hemet-San Jacinto Valley, then through the Sage area where my father owned a small ranch, and on through Aguanga and Oak Grove to the Warner Ranch. In the latter part of the 1890's, but mainly in the very early 1900's, my brothers and I would go to meet the Vail herds, and enjoy riding with them for awhile. Usually, after these droves of cattle would pass through the area, especially after a sizeable herd had been moved, some of them would be lost along the way as they slipped out of the herd in very brushy places, or perhaps left behind because of being unable to travel with the herd.

Sam Taylor was then foreman on the Warner Ranch, so he and one or two of his cowboys would come and stay at our place while getting the stragglers together. My brothers and I would again enjoy riding with Taylor and his men, and usually we knew where to find most of the cattle.

Many years after the Fox boy was shot at Carrizo Creek, and at a time when I was working for the Vail Company on the Pauba

Ranch at Temecula, I met Ed Vail, whom his nephew, Mahlon Vail, and other members of the Walter Vail family called "Tio", meaning *uncle* in Spanish.

While visiting with Mr. Vail, I learned that he had kept a diary of the cattle drive in 1886, from the Empire Ranch to the Warner, and when speaking of the shooting of the Fox boy, I could tell that he, like other old-timers whom I heard talk about the incident, felt that the shooting of the boy had not been at all necessary.

I saw the Fox boy's grave for the first time in 1910, when on a cattle drive over the old Butterfield Stage Route to Imperial Valley, and as I sat upon my horse looking down at the grave, I could not help but feel the disarmed young man had been murdered. Even though he was no doubt guilty of having stolen some horses, I felt that I would much rather have been the boy who had made the mistake of stealing horses, than to have been the man who shot him.

It is my understanding that some time after the Fox boy was buried at Carrizo Creek, someone placed a marker at the grave bearing this inscription: "Joe Fox, Age 19, Murdered." In the latter part of the 1930's I drove my car out to Carrizo Creek from Imperial Valley and photographed the grave. The reproduction is shown in these pages. I have been told that the grave has since been destroyed.

Frank Clark, his saddle and pack horses, at the Joel Reed place in 1903. (Harry Bergman collection)

Frank Clark cattle camp in Borrego Valley Ocotillo fence built by author's brother, Albe "Zeke" Reed. (Reed collection)

Frank Clark kneeling at right, Fred Clark standing at horse's head. William Dyke and an unidentified cowboy loading pack animals. (Photo from the Harry Bergman collection, taken at Coyote Canyon cattle camp about 1905.)

CHAPTER 3

OLD-TIME CATTLEMEN AND COWBOYS
OF ANZA BORREGO

THE CLARK brothers (Frank and Fred) were well-known cattlemen of Coyote Canyon, Borrego Valley, and of course, Clark Lake was named for these two cattlemen. I do not know for sure what year the Clark brothers went into the Anza-Borrego Desert the first time, but the reproduction presented in these pages of the transfer of title to lands at La Puerta (Laporto) from Pisqual to F. S. Clark, bears the date of January 6, 1891, so it is reasonable to believe they started their operations on the desert about that time.

The lands that were transferred from Pisqual to F.S. Clark are situated at the head of Nance Canyon, one of the tributaries leading to what is now referred to as the Turkey Track, forming the head of Coyote Canyon. Fred resided on this land until the 1930's. He was born in Indiana, and he passed away in December, 1938, at the age of 79. The site of the old Fred Clarke adobe is now referred to as San Carlos Pass, but it was known to the old-timers as La Puerta, having the meaning to them as the Door of the Desert.

Frank Clark filed a homestead claim about six miles to the West of where Fred settled. This land is in what the old-timers called Durazno Valley, the word *durazno* being Spanish for "peach" or "peach tree." Frank resided at this location until his death in December, 1937. His daughter, Lola, still lives on the old homestead with her husband, Howard Bailey, where they are still in the cattle business. Some of the Bailey cattle still winter in Coyote Canyon where they own a very large acreage of land. Beside the daughter, Lola, there is a son, Vermal, who now resides in San Jacinto, Calif.

When Frank and Fred Clark first began their search on the

The old Fred Clark adobe at La Puerta, at the head of Nance Canyon, a tributary of Coyote Canyon. (Collection of Mrs. Arthur Cary.)

desert for possible cattle-range where water could be developed, they traveled on foot, taking along a burro to carry water, food, and a light bedroll. Frank related to me the story of a trip he and Fred made around to the east of the Old Santa Rosa Mountain (Santa Rosa Vieja) when they came very near to perishing from thirst. I cannot remember the story in detail as Frank told it to me, but Fred became so ill from the effects of thirst that he had to quit trying to travel any farther, so he stayed in the shade of steep canyon walls while Frank continued following up a wash—desert canyon—in search of the water they and the burro so desperately needed. Frank was fortunate enough to find a wet spot in the sand where he could dig and obtain enough water to quench his own thirst, water the burro, and fill the canteen to take back to Fred. Frank's extra stamina and determination no doubt was what saved the life of Fred, and as I remember the story, Frank could not have held out much longer, and the situation was desperate enough for them that Fred never cared to talk about it.

When the Clark brothers found the water at Clark Lake, they had decided to try digging at a spot where they thought the water should be the most likely to be not too many feet below the surface of the ground. The spot they decided upon was to the northeast of the barren lake bottom, where there were some mesquite trees, and right near where there now stands the home of one of the homesteaders. Much of the day had gone by when they started to dig with pick and shovel, and just before dark, at a depth of about thirteen feet, they found sufficient water to serve themselves and the burros for the night.

After finding the water so near the surface, they then started plans to get equipment and well-casing to the location to try putting down a well from which they could pump water for cattle. Transportation in the days of the old-timers of the desert was quite a problem, and the principal means for getting equipment and materials for the well the Clark brothers now planned were two burros, Pete and Leechy, and an old Mexican *carreta* to which they worked a horse by the name of Mack.

When using the *carreta,* the route of travel after passing out of Coyote Canyon, was to follow down the main wash near the foot of Butler Mountain (Coyote Mountain) to where the Pegleg Monument now stands, then to the east just about as the road now runs into Clark Lake. With packs on the burros, the route traveled after passing out of Coyote Canyon, was to follow the Old Indian Trail that leads across the steep rough ridge that extends to the north from Butler Mountain, and is just about due east from the old "Doc" Beaty Place (De Anza Ranch). Near the top of the ridge, the old trail leads between two large boulders that are so close together that the short-legged burros had to be unpacked before leading them through. The procedure of unpacking and repacking required so much time, that some of the old-timers argued it would be just as well to travel the same route around Butler Mountain as was traveled with the Mexican *carreta.*

The equipment for the work on the well consisted of a tripod made of metal waterpipe; a single pulley fastened to the top of the tripod; a sand bucket fastened to the end of the rope, the rope then passed through the pulley. To push the casing into the ground was a beam made of two 2x12s, fastened together far enough apart, so that when the beam was placed with the two-inch surfaces on the top and the bottom, it could then rest upon a steel collar designed to push the casing into the ground. One end of the beam was fastened solidly to a weight buried in the ground near where the casing was to be, the outer end of the beam was elevated by raising it with a second tripod and double pulleys. The tripod for the operation of the sand bucket was then placed directly over where the well was to be, the sand bucket passed between the 2x12s of the beam, then through the steel collar and into the casing. The sand bucket was then operated by one or two men using the rope and single pulley to raise the bucket from the bottom, then suddenly releasing the rope so that the weight of the steel bucket would strike the bottom with enough force to cause more sand to enter the bucket through the valve at the bottom. Very crude equipment for sure, but could it be that the well drilling machinery of today, is at least, in part, the manifestation of ideas developed through the use of such crude equipment?

After the well was completed, water was pumped into a trough by two methods—the old hand pump, and the other method was to hitch one of the burros to a long sweep, and by the animal traveling in a circle the pumping chore was done. This, of course, must have been very monotonous for the burro, even though he is noted for what appears to be unlimited patience as long as he is given plenty of time.

Through the years following the establishment of the cattle-camp at Clark Lake, there were of course, a number of old-time cowboys who worked with cattle being wintered on the desert and watering at the well. Those with whom I was acquainted as a boy were: Celso Serano—an Indian; a colored boy by the name of Dan Grant, Archie Daugherty, and Sylvester (Sal) Biles.

Some time after the well was put in operation, Frank Clark became interested in the story an old Indian at Rockhouse Valley told about the Indians digging into the sand not too far from what is now Font's Point and having enough water for one of their camps when gathering food from the area. Frank made an appointment for the Indian to meet him at the cattle-camp, and when the Indian arrived at the camp he was traveling on foot in making the trip from Rockhouse Valley. Frank noticed when the Indian was coming to the camp that he lifted his feet rather high at each step and wondered why. He was wearing sandals, so by lifting his feet higher than usual, he prevented scooping up sand at each step.

Frank had agreed to pay the Indian ten dollars to show the location of the water, but so many years had passed since being there, the old fellow failed to locate the place. However, typical of Frank Clark, the Indian returned to Rockhouse Valley with the ten dollars in his pocket. It is thought the Indian traveled one of the old foot trails across the mountain into Clark Valley, instead of going around by Hidden Spring. I have intended to try to find the trail the Indian was thought to have traveled on his mission to show Clark the water, but I never did get around to carrying out the idea.

Often Frank and Fred Clark would have a camp at the Joel Reed homestead in Coyote Canyon, and Howard Bailey tells of stop-

Fred Clark at La Puerta near the De Anza marker. (Mrs. Arthur Cary collection)

ping at the Joel Reed place one time when the Indian—Celso Serano—was staying there for the Clarks. When Howard rode up to the camp, Celso wanted to know if he could tell him the time of day, what month it was, and what year. Celso stated that all he knew about it was that the day was Sunday. Sunday was his day off, so he kept track of that, but evidently could not be bothered with the lesser importance of time.

When warm weather came on, and it was time for the cattle to go back to the mountains, they were gathered from Clark Lake area into Coyote Canyon. Many of the cattle would work through the canyon of their own free will without being driven, and during the latter part of the cattle gathering procedure, the camp would be at Fig Tree (Upper Willows).

In later years, when the homesteaders started coming into Borrego Valley, Frank bought a piece of land near the center of Borrego Valley that had a well on it, and it was there that he established the main cattle camp.

Frank's son, Vermal, tells about one night when he and some others were traveling after night on the desert with the pack animal in the lead the dust seemed unusually bad and caused them to keep sneezing. The following morning the mystery of the dust being so unusually bad was solved when sorting out the food in the pack, they found that the lid was off the pepper can. When the pack animal would trot, the pepper would leak through the bottom of the pack box and become a part of the dust.

Fred Clark never married, and he did not stay in the cattle business to the end of his life as did Frank. I believe it was somewhere about 1905 that he sold his cattle to William Tripp, but he continued to raise horses. A number of his horses were either blue or red roans, and were the toughest horses to stand hard work I have ever known. A man needed to be a better than average rider to keep one of them between his knees when they decided you had been on his back long enough, and to outrun one of them, you needed to be mounted on a fair race horse.

Fred Clark possessed a sense of humor peculiar to himself. One time when at the Aguanga store, about twenty or twenty-five miles distant from his ranch, he asked the owner of the store—George Smith—if he wanted to buy some empty beer bottles, and Smith told him to bring down what he had. A few days later, Fred arrived at the Aguanga Store in a two-horse ranch wagon, using a twelve-inch board placed across the front end of the wagon bed to serve as a seat. Fred stopped in front of the store to ask Smith where he wanted the bottles, and of course, when Smith came out to see the wagon bed loaded to capacity with beer bottles, was the moment Fred had been looking forward to. Smith's face registered amazement, but he told Fred where to unload them. When Fred casually told Smith he would get the rest of his supply down "right soon," Smith paid for the wagon load already delivered, but advised that he could not use the rest of such a plentiful supply.

In those days deer were plentiful in Southern California, so there were persons who liked to go to Fred Clark's Ranch to hunt and drink beer, so over a period of a number of years, a fair supply of beer bottles had accumulated. I do not remember if Fred ever found a market for the rest of his beer bottles. It is very likely another store or two could have been flooded.

At another time, after Frank bought the land and well in Borrego Valley, Fred went out with Frank and someone else to search for a land corner stake, but after a short time Fred apparently became disinterested and sat down. After quite some time had passed, and the other men were going to give up the search for the stake, Fred called and wanted to know just what it was they were trying to find. When they told him he said in his high-pitched voice: "Why didn't you fellers say so! I been sittin' on it here all the time!!"

After the Model T Ford came into the picture, and Frank had

his cattle camp in Borrego Valley, he claimed to have planted the longest row of pink beans ever known in the area. Starting for the cattle camp, he had placed a paper bag of beans on the floor of the Ford, between the seats; when he arrived at the camp, the paper bag was just about empty, with a small hole in the bottom. After a rain that fell a few days later, bean vines began to appear in the dirt road all the way from where Highway 78 passes through the Narrows to the cattle camp near the center of Borrego Valley—a distance of several miles. Evidently, the rough dirt road kept the Ford bouncing around enough to keep the beans dropping through the bottom.

JOHN McCAIN

JOHN McCAIN was among the very first of the cattlemen, and could have been the first to come into the Borrego Valley area. His cabin was just across the wash to the southwest of the Old Borrego Spring where the Borrego Valley narrows down to the wash that leads to the dry lake at Ocotillo Well on Highway 78. The last time I was at his old cabin site there were a few boards, or pieces of boards

John McCain cabin and cattle corral near Old Borrego Spring.

John McCain was one of the earliest cattlemen to live in the Borrego area. This picture was taken at the old Vallecito Stage Station. (Collection of Mrs. Edyth McGowan)

Nattie Blanchard walking behind a wagon on the old Plum Canyon road that the McCain brothers built. (Howard Bailey collection)

rather, still scattered around on the ground. Near by was evidence of a hole where John would get water during the more rainy years, but the Old Borrego Spring across the wash was the permanent water. Since so much recent pumping of water in the Borrego Valley, the old spring no longer flows. This spring was one of the watering places upon which the Indians, and the old-timers could depend, although the water was very poor in quality.

The first time I visited Old Borrego Spring was just two or three days before Christmas of 1913 when my brother, Gilbert (Gib) and I were riding through on horseback from Imperial Valley to spend the holidays with our parents at the Mud Spring Ranch about 15 miles southeast of Hemet. Since early boyhood, I had heard old-timers talk about Borrego Springs water, so thought I would try it. As I have said many times before, I found it to taste but very little better than the treated water we are expected to drink today.

This first time I was at the spring, there was an old wooden watering trough sitting flat on the ground from which several saddle horses or work stock could be watered, and, of course, a few head of cattle.

I have been informed by other old-timers of the desert, that it was John McCain and a brother who built the old road from Sentenac Cienega, up over the hill, and then down Plum Canyon to join the Grapevine Canyon Road at Yaqui Well.

I have a tape recording from Mrs. Edyth McGowan, who is the youngest daughter of John McCain, and is still living at Julian, where she was Postmistress for 35 years. At the age of 79, Mrs. Edyth McGowan is the only one still living of the John McCain family of five children—two sons and three daughters.

Mrs. McGowan was unable to tell me what year her father first went to Borrego Valley, but I did receive information that he sold his land there to Charlie Potter, an old-timer of the San Diego County area. From Mrs. Edyth McGowan I learned that her father and mother (Mary E. Cline) were married in Mesa Grande, California, after making the trip from the Old Vallecito Stage Station on horseback. This marriage ceremony was performed by Judge Leslie on August 22, 1872, and they first lived at Vallecito where Mrs. John Hart was a niece of John McCain, and was the widow of John Hart who was buried at Vallecito about the middle of March, 1867.

Through the tape recording, Mrs. McGowan informs that her father was born in Little Rock, Arkansas, December 4, 1876, and came to California with an ox team when he was the age of 12. He first became a blacksmith by trade, and in later years, beside being in the cattle business, he drove a jerkline mule team from San

Diego to Julian for a number of years. Also, at one time he carried the mail from Julian to Warner Springs with two horses and a spring wagon.

John McCain was a large powerful man who well knew the ways of outdoor life with horses and cattle, and could always make the best of whatever situation lay at hand. Judd Tripp tells of seeing him at a celebration in Julian one time when running his horse past a fifty pound sack of flour, McCain caught the sack with one hand and jerked the fifty pounds into the saddle with him. Quite a feat to accomplish from the back of a running horse, and if you do not believe it, just give the stunt a try.

In line with John McCain's way of life, and making the best of whatever situation lay at hand, Howard Bailey tells of coming past Old Borrego Spring one time when John was giving a little boy a bath in the watering trough, and using a gunny sack to wipe the little fellow off with. The life of John McCain, and the family history would make quite a story by itself, but if I were qualified to try to write it up, space at this time would not permit. John McCain passed away January 12, 1948.

TRIPP BROTHERS

The winter of 1897-98 was an extremely dry one in Southern California, so the Tripp brothers (Shasta and William) like many other cattlemen, were desperately in search of some means by which they might at least save part of their cattle. Their home ranches were at what is still known as Tripp Flats, a few miles to the northeast of what is now known as the Anza Valley, and about twenty miles southeast of Hemet, California.

Grass and browse conditions were so poor at their ranches, they knew it was useless to try to keep stock there, so they went to the desert to try to find a way to solve their problem. At Mason Valley, in the Anza-Borrego Desert, they made a deal with Mr. Mason to take two hundred and sixty head there to try to save them from starvation. At best, it was quite a gamble, but they knew of nothing better, and should the rains come early, it was a better chance than at the ranch.

(Above) Charlie Ticknor, one of the cow boys who helped the Tripp brothers on the 1897 cattle drive to Mason Valley (Collection of the author)

(Left) S. V. Tripp, standing and his son Shasta. S. V. Tripp was the author's grandfather.

The cowboys who drove the cattle were Judd Tripp (a younger brother to William and Shasta), Jimmy Stephens, Charlie Ticknor, a man by the name of Addison, and William Tripp. Ozro Tripp, another brother, drove the chuck wagon. Jimmie Stephens and Charlie Ticknor stayed at Mason Valley to get the cattle settled while the other men went back to the ranch.

William Tripp, Judd Tripp, and Julio Montes went right back to the desert on their way to Borrego Valley where they had planned to make a watering place in preparation for taking a smaller herd of cattle there for the winter. They traveled by way of San Felipe Ranch to gather a few head of cattle they had left there out of the herd they took to Mason Valley. With team and wagon they were hauling a slip scraper for the building of the watering place. When leaving the San Felipe Valley, the shortest route for them to travel with the wagon was from the Sentenac Cienega, up over the old wagon road leading to the east from the Cienega, and after crossing the rocky hill the road then lead down Plum Canyon to Yaqui Well where they intended to stay for the night because of the few poor cattle they were driving.

Upon arrival at Yaqui Well, they found there were seven or eight dead jack rabbits floating on top of the water. The well at that time was about eight feet deep, and they had the task of cleaning out the water, the dead jack rabbits, and thoroughly scraping down the sides of the well and throwing out the dirt. At the present time—January 1963—when Judd—at the age of 86—is telling of this experience, he has this to say: "The water that came into the well after cleaning wasn't so bad at that".

Upon arrival in Borrego Valley with the small bunch of cattle, they were taken to the water at Old Borrego Spring, and the site picked for making a watering place and cow-camp for the winter was about half way between Old-Borrego Spring and where Eddie DuVall's Borego Store now stands. With a slip scraper and team of horses—two horses—quite a large hole was made where the water was very near to the surface in the days of the old-timers. Three sides of the hole were fenced off so that the cattle could get to the water from only one side where boards were built up to serve as a watering trough.

While William Tripp, Judd Tripp, and Julio Montes were preparing the watering place, Charlie Ticknor came on horseback from Mason Valley where he had laid over to help Jimmie Stephens get the cattle settled to the situation there where they were to remain for the winter.

The route over which Charlie Ticknor had traveled en route from Mason Valley was through Box Canyon, Blair Valley, and then leaving the old Butterfield Stage Route he followed an old Indian trail out of Earthquake Valley, and then down Mine Canyon to where Tamarisk Camp-ground now stands, and from there he followed the old Yaqui Pass Indian Trail into Borrego Valley to contact the Tripps and Julio Montes at the new cattle camp and watering place. Signs of these old trails could still be found in 1958 when I traveled over the old route on horseback.

The night that Charlie Ticknor arrived at the Tripp Cow-Camp in Borrego Valley, Frank and Fred Clark were there on their way to Fish Creek near the present site of the old Harper's Well. The Clark brothers were in search of more water and range where they could go with drouth-stricken cattle.

The following morning Charlie Ticknor went with Frank and Fred Clark on their trip to Fish Creek in search of more cattle range. Upon arrival at the Fish Creek water, they soon learned the quicksand made it too treacherous a place to take poor cattle, so the idea was abandoned.

As I have stated before, I often meet with persons who ask why anyone would go to the desert with cattle. When the Clarks and Tripps were so desperately in search of a place to take drouth-stricken cattle, the range supplements we know about today were

William B. Tripp, cattleman and prospector in the Anza-Borrego area, named Butler Mountain in the 1880s. (Edith Tripp Reed collection)

Ozro Tripp, one of several Tripp Brothers, founded the Three Buttes Mine, later known as the Ghost Mine. (Clyde Tripp collection)

not at all available to them. Going to the desert with cattle in those days could be a good gamble if the rains there came early, but when the rains failed to come the gamble on the desert could turn out to be a poor one. I know of no place where cattle will fatten faster than on the desert when the flowers come as the camera fans hope to find them in these days of automobiles and surfaced roads. I never have sold fatter cattle than some I sold out of Borrego one year in the month of April, and this same year "Billie" Moore of Riverside bought a car load of cows from Frank Clark that were fattened in Borrego, and he spoke of them as being too fat.

When the Tripps finished their watering place in Borrego Valley, they went back to their ranch by way of Coyote Canyon, and in the tape recording I have from Judd, he refers to the trip through Coyote Canyon with team and wagon as being a difficult and rough one. The Coyote Canyon Route in those days, and at an earlier date when my father went into the canyon with his cart drawn by two oxen, was quite a different story from what the members of the Jeep Cavalcade experience each year at the present time.

Even as late as in the 1920's, when in a Model T Ford with Ruxtel axle, over sized tires on the rear wheels, and with Johnie Taylor mounted on a thirteen hundred pound horse helping by pulling on a rope attached to the front axle of the Ford, I found it not to be what could be called a day off in getting from the Joel Reed place to the Narrows about half a mile below the Fig Tree (Upper Willows). On the Ford I was hauling some baled hay and rolled barley for the cow-camp at Fig Tree, while gathering cattle and getting them out of the Coyote Canyon area. Incidentally, the

Judd Tripp, more than 80 years old, re-visited the Carrizo Creek recently. (Photo by author)

Chester Tripp as a boy drove the supply wagon to the Three Buttes Mine years ago. (Photo by author)

Johnie Taylor who helped me was a grandson of the John Taylor who arrived at Carrizo Creek with ox teams and covered wagons on October 12, 1864, when on his way from Comanche County, Texas, to Southern California.

At the Narrows below Fig Tree, my brother "Zeke" Reed met us with pack animals to take the hay and grain to the cow-camp, and at that time drivers of jeeps would have experienced some very strenuous exercise in getting jeeps through the large boulders along the bottom of the canyon. During the winter of 1926 and 1927 I saw a stream of water running through Borrego Valley from Coyote Canyon, and another out of Palm Creek into the Valley that were of unbelievable proportions. Such flood conditions can make even jeep travel very difficult in places along the way through Coyote Canyon. Old-timers of the desert would never make camp in the washes during stormy weather.

Upon returning to the ranch after having prepared the watering place in Borrego Valley, the Tripp brothers gathered the remainder of their cattle—something less than one hundred head—and drove them down Coyote Canyon to Borrego Valley for the winter. The evening they arrived in Borrego with the cattle, it started snowing, and the following morning about four inches of snow covered the ground. Due to a very hard wind that was blowing, they experienced a very difficult time in trying to keep warm in an open camp.

Enough moisture fell before the storm was over that the water level in the watering place was caused to rise, and the water then became so roiled from cattle walking in it outside the board wall that it became necessary to put down a well to pump water from it into a watering trough as the Clarks were doing at their camp.

When time came for the gathering of the cattle to take them back to the ranch in the mountains, the cattle in Borrego had done very well, but in Mason Valley the story was quite different. When they finished gathering the cattle in Mason Valley, just about one hundred of them had died, and some of those that survived the winter were still very thin.

Here again I wish to say that as we see the cattle business today, it is very difficult to understand why cattlemen would take a chance on going to the desert with their stock when in search of relief from drouth conditions. In the days of the old-time cattlemen, transportation facilities were quite different from what they are at the present time. There were no trucks or surfaced roads in those times; no range supplements or feed lots as we have at the present time; and marketing possibilities in drouth times could

Cowboys on the Tripp Brothers 1909 cattle drive through Coyote Canyon to Imperial Valley. Left to right: "Gib" Reed, "Chuck" Tripp, third and fourth unidentified, William Tripp, Quinn Davidson, "Pete" Hibbert, and "Sal" Biles. (Collection of the author)

be almost impossible for cattlemen of certain areas. Even in my time, I have sold fat cows for two and one half cents per pound, and fat steers for three dollars and forty cents per hundred.

In the early 1900's, when Imperial Valley was beginning to be a winter feeding ground, was when the Tripps and others started making cattle-drives through the Anza-Borrego Desert area to the pasture lands of Imperial Valley. In the fall of 1909, Tripp brothers made their first cattle-drive to Imperial Valley by way of Coyote Canyon, Borrego Valley, Old Borrego Spring, Fish Creek water (in vicinity of Harper's Well), and Kane Spring. In this herd of cattle were renegade steers of at least twelve years that the Tripps had purchased from Fred Clark, and from the Hamilton Brothers (Joe and Henry) of the Anza area.

Of the ten men driving this herd of cattle, I know of only three who are still living in the year 1963. They are: Judd Tripp at the age of 86; Charlie Tripp, well up in his 70's; and Sylvester "Sal" Biles, who is also getting near the 80 mark. Judd Tripp was not with the cattle on the way down Coyote Canyon, but met them at Old Borrego Spring with the chuck wagon after traveling the old route down Grapevine Canyon, and then following the old John McCain wagon road to Old Borego Springs. There Shasta Tripp took over the job of driving chuck-wagon and being the cook. There were two young men with this cattle drive of whom

I am not quite sure as to their identity, but I believe they were Dexter Jones and Stanley Shaw. Of those on this cattle drive whom I know have passed away are: William Tripp, Shasta Tripp, my brother Gilbert ("Gib") Reed, my brother-in-law (Quin Davidson), Pete Hibbert, and Archie Daugherty.

———————————◄•►———————————

SYLVESTER "SAL" BILES

"SAL" BILES, as he is still known to all his friends—of whom there are many—arrived in the Anza-Borrego Desert in 1900. "Sal" went from the San Jacinto area of Riverside County in Southern California, to stay at the cow-camp at Clark Lake, where an Indian cowboy, Celso Serano, was staying for the Clark brothers. At that time, "Sal" was a big, husky and energetic boy, who liked to pester someone as pastime, so one day when he was really having a great time bothering Celso, and not heeding the Indian's warnings that he had better behave himself, "Sal" eventually found that the big Indian meant what he said, and he found himself tied to a mesquite tree near the camp. "Sal" was very well versed in just about all the "cuss" words, so Celso really had the opportunity to listen, and to watch "Sal's" struggle to get loose. Most of the day had passed by when Celso evidently decided the boy had learned his lesson and turned him loose. Celso was an experienced cowboy in tying up bronco cattle and horses, so I am quite confident that "Sal" became convinced the big Indian knew just how to tie up a boy so that he would stay. The last time I was at the site of the Clark Well, the old mesquite tree had died, so I told "Sal", that in my mind, the tree had died from the damage done to it during his struggle and efforts to get loose.

For quite a number of years Biles felt that the only home he had was with Frank Clark in Durazno Valley, where he worked for Frank with the cattle, and of course would go to the desert in the winter time. One winter or spring when "Sal" was riding after cattle on the desert, one of the horses he used—a mare named Snip—became tender footed, so he left her with a man by the name of Ebens who said he would take her to the ranch at Durazno Valley to be shod. Ebens had a cabin between Joel Reed's

Place and what is now known as De Anza Ranch, and for quite some time he owned quite a number of hogs that ranged along the Coyote Creek and at times pretty well out into the Borrego Valley.

A few days after "Sal" left the horse with Ebens to be taken to the ranch to be shod, he dropped by to pick her up, but found the animal had not been taken to the ranch, but instead the man Ebens had taken her to the Wilson Store, and without her being shod had used her to pack back a supply of groceries. Immediately, in no uncertain terms, "Sal" was explaining to Ebens just what he thought of a man who would break a trust and use a sorefooted animal in his betrayal. Ebens then hurried into his cabin, and when he returned to the door carrying a 30-30 carbine rifle, he was knocked down by a box "Sal" used from where he stood in readiness beside the door. Eben's rifle was then thrown into the creek, and he had become very well tamed to the situation.

Evidently, Biles and Ebens were destined to be a bit more on "neighborly" terms than most people, for at a later date when Biles was passing by Ebens' place he saw his wagon in the yard that he had bought from a well driller farther down in the Borrego Valley. Biles informed Ebens that the wagon belonged to him, and that he was coming back to get it. When Biles went to get the wagon it was gone from the Ebens place, but it was found at the Wilson Store on San Felipe. Biles put a pair of harnesses on one of his horses and rode the other to the Wilson Store and brought

Sylvester "Sal" Biles, one of the early-day Borrego ranchers and cow-hands. (Collection of the Biles family)

Theodore Ebens standing in front of his cabin near the mouth of Coyote Canyon. (Howard Bailey collection)

his wagon back as promised, and this resulted in there being some pretty loud talk from Ebens as to what was going to happen to "Sal", but had Ebens known "Sal" Biles as well as I do, he would not have expected him to be frightened.

One winter when "Sal" was staying in the Joel Reed Valley and staying in Joel's cabin, a slender pale faced young fellow came to the cabin and stayed a couple of nights. The young fellow walked into the area by way of Indian Canyon, and of course had no trouble in finding a place to stay when arriving at the Clark cow-camp. Noticing that the young fellow was carrying but very little with him, "Sal" offered to share his bed, but was thanked in rather an embarrassed manner and assured he would fare well on the dirt floor beside the bed.

When the young fellow left he traveled the trail back into Indian Canyon, and while Biles was absent from the camp a few days his food supply disappeared. When officers came to investigate the whyfores of the young fellow being in the area, they found that Biles' "boy friend" was a girl. After this discovery, Biles' "friends" never missed an opportunity to remind him of the incident. I never did learn what became of the girl after the officers made their investigation.

In 1912 Biles took care of a sizable herd of cattle that a man by the name of Rankin brought into Borrego Valley. Rankin's cow-camp was at Frenche's Well not far from where Ed DuVall's Old-Borego Store now stands. Frenche's Well flowed a small stream of artesian water from which many of the Rankin cattle were watered. One day while Biles was working for Rankin, he had been quite a number of hours without water, so when passing the old abandoned Tripp camp he decided he had been long enough without a drink and would try the water there. The horse refused to drink, but "Sal" thought it good enough for him as thirsty as he was. Soon after drinking the water he became very ill, and from what he says about it now, I take for granted that he was just about as ill as he has ever been.

While camping at Frenche's Well, Biles old "neighbor", Ebens, came along with nine pack burros and stayed overnight with him. Ebens was very friendly, so the old hatchet of the past was buried, and if I remember correctly, this was the last time the old Borrego Valley "neighbors" ever met.

Biles and his wife (Treasure) now reside where Highway 79 crosses the cattle-guard on the North boundary of Warner Ranch, at what was known to the old-timers as the Jim Holcolm Place, where Treasure Biles' parents, (The Jeffries), lived for many years.

"Sal" and Treasure have only one child (a son) who lives at Upland, California, where he is with the National Guard.

In the summer of 1960, Biles and I went up into Inyo County and helped a friend by the name of Mark Lacey gather his cattle off the desert and take them into the High Sierras for the summer. During the summer of 1961 the Lacey's insurance company decided that Biles and I are too far past 21 to be on the payroll. However, the Laceys changed to another Company and had me back to help last summer and asked me to call Biles and tell him they would like to have him go, too, but he had made some other plans. Biles and I are nearing the end of the time that we can be "wild" cowboys, but we have both enjoyed many experiences in the cattle-world of the past, that, because of changing times, will not be a part of the lives of the young cowboys of today. However, the young cowboys of today can handle trucks and trailers on freeways and other places of heavy traffic where Biles and I must be too wise to venture.

In 1912 "Sal" Biles was in charge of a herd of desert longhorns belonging to a man named Rankin. The cow camp was at Frenche's Well. (Photo from the Biles collection)

JUDD TRIPP

JUDD TRIPP is one of the very few of the old-timers of the desert still living in 1963. On October 19, 1962, he reached his 86th birthday, and he still enjoys relating old-time experiences in the Anza-Borrego Desert. It is amazing how well he remembers names and incidents one would think he would have forgotten years ago. He traveled over the old Butterfield Stage Route between Imperial Valley and Temecula quite a number of times. Sometimes driving cattle, sometimes just traveling through on horseback, and at other times traveling with team and light wagon.

Judd tells of people years ago believing that there were ghosts at Vallecito, and says that perhaps the story got started because of the graves there. One night, about 2 A.M., when stopping at the old wayside watering trough to give his saddle-horse a drink, she suddenly raised her head to look at something white that darted from the mesquite thicket. Judd states that he never did believe in ghosts, but admits that just for an instant he was startled. The white object proved to be a dog belonging to some people traveling through with team and wagon.

In 1910 when Judd was coming back across the desert after a cattle-drive to Imperial Valley, he saw three antelope just before arriving at the Carrizo Creek water, and those were the last antelope I know of anyone's seeing in the area. He tells of a time years ago when a cowboy by the name of Jim Lowe roped an antelope at Sentenac Cienega. The antelope had just been to the water, so was at a disadvantage in its effort to get away. Incidentally, when I was in New Mexico in 1938, I saw a young cowboy catch an antelope on a young buckskin horse. He was an experienced wild horse hunter, so did not run his horse off his feet as the old-timers would say, and knew when to take advantage of the contour of the ground, and give the horse the advantage. He told me that if I knew of anyone with a gambling spirit who thought it could not be done, to bring them over, for he would like to have a new Ford, and would bet up to twelve hundred dollars he could catch a buck antelope.

I have a tape recording from Judd Tripp relating a trip he and a man by the name of Davis made on the desert in April of 1898 when they were in search of a place that would be a good cattle range. This was the year that his brothers, Will and Shasta, had cattle in the Mason Valley, so he and Davis stayed overnight at the Tripp Cow-Camp, where what cattle had survived the winter were being gathered to take back to the mountains.

The following day when Judd and Davis arrived at Carrizo Creek, they met with two men and a boy who were on their way to Cibola on the Arizona side of the Colorado River not so very far from Ehrenburg. One of these men knew the desert well, so Judd and Davis decided to follow them on a shortcut they intended to take after passing over the very steep old Blue Hill Grade and onto the mesa that slopes toward Salton Sea. Of course, the Colorado River had not yet broken into what is now Imperial Valley and re-filled the Salton Sea, so the shortcut across to the Southern Pacific Railroad was then possible.

After leaving the Butterfield Stage Route to take the short-cut, they traveled to a place Judd refers to as Clear Lake where they camped for the night. Judd and Davis were traveling with a light spring wagon drawn by two horses, and they were leading a third horse to ride or to work in place of either of the other two should one become lame or need rest for some other reason. The following night they camped at a place mentioned as the Pot Holes where they again had water for the horses.

By this time they had learned the shortcut was easily followed because of the tracks of other wagons having been over the route ahead of them. The spring wagon in which they were traveling was much lighter than the wagon of the two men and the boy, so realizing the lighter wagon could make much better time than could the heavier one, Judd and Davis decided to go on ahead. They made a dry camp before reaching the railroad, but when they arrived at Glamis the following day, water was available for the horses at ten cents per head, and the railroad employees gave them what drinking water they needed. The water at Glamis had been hauled in by railroad water tanks.

After leaving Glamis, the next camping place was on the Colorado River where, of course, water was no problem, and there was some grass for the horses. Traveling up the California side of the river they arrived at a cattle-camp belonging to a man by the name of Frank Hodges, and there they met Gail Lewis and Jim Haslam, who had a small boat they used for crossing over the river into Arizona. Jim Haslam was an old-timer of the desert areas whom I knew from early boyhood, and he married a girl by the name of Oaty Crawford with whom I went to grammar school when in the first grade. I attended Jim's funeral services in Hemet about three years ago, and the wife still lives at Vallevista, not far from Hemet and San Jacinto.

Judd Tripp and Davis made a deal with Jim Haslam and Gail Lewis to cross them over the river into Arizona. The horses were crossed one at a time by leading them behind the boat. The first one was very much afraid of the water and gave considerable trouble; the second one crossed easily enough, and the third one being very anxious to get to the other horses, swam high out of the water, and with her head over the rear of the boat, pushed hard enough that very little rowing was necessary. The spring wagon and supplies were crossed on the boat.

After getting across the river they traveled up the Arizona side to Ehrenburg, and found nothing of interest to them there, so they traveled east to a mining camp where a man had a general store and traded supplies to the miners for their gold. By this time the finding of a place to run cattle seemed very unlikely to them, so they started toward Yuma intending to cross back over the river there and start back toward home.

The first night on the way to Yuma, they made camp near a place known as Black Tanks, where, by digging into the sand, they had plenty of water for the horses and for themselves. The next camping place was on the river at a place called Castle Dome Landing near the Castle Dome Mine. Out on the river was an old boat named Mojave that brought supplies to the landing. Often the boat was rather difficult to land because of the shifting channel, so Indians were hired to wade out into the river to locate the channel and serve as guides for the skipper of the boat.

After leaving Castle Dome Landing in the morning, they arrived at Yuma fairly early in the afternoon, and camped over night, intending to cross the river the following morning. There was no wagon bridge over the river at that time, so they had to drive the team and wagon onto the ferry boat to get across, for which they paid a fee of five dollars.

Soon after leaving Yuma they had to cross over the Mexican Border in order to detour to the south of the sand dunes through which there was not yet a road. A Mexican officer inspected their belongings at the border, and they traveled that day to Seven Wells where the water holes were shallow and the water was very strong with alkali. The horses would drink the water, but Judd speaks of this water being hard for them to take.

From Seven Wells they traveled to what had been referred to them as Buzzards Well, and Judd wonders if this could have been what the earlier travelers of the route referred to as Indian Wells. I wonder if it could have been what John Taylor referred to as Alamo Well. However, Judd refers to the water as being very good, and served them well after having the bad water at Seven Wells.

The next camping place was at Cameron Lake where the water was very low, and was so salty that the horses would not drink, and the coffee made with this water Judd mentions as being just about impossible. From Cameron Lake they went to a place named Laguna where there were still the remains of an old stage station, and here again they were relieved to find the water good.

Instead of continuing their way home by way of Carrizo, they turned off on the road to Campo by way of Coyote Well, where they made camp for the night and cut galleta grass to feed to the horses. From Coyote Wells the old wagon road led them through Devil's Canyon, and Judd relates that this strip of the road had been well named, for it had been washed out so that it was difficult to travel over even with the light spring wagon.

Arriving at Jacumba they had finished their travels in the desert areas, so the trip was completed by traveling through Julian and Warner Ranch on the way to their homes near Aguanga on what is now Highway 79, running through Hemet and joining Highway 60 near Beaumont.

Judd is one of three brothers and one sister of my mother's who are still living at this writing, January 11, 1963. He never married, and for quite a number of years he has resided near Sultana, Tulare County, California. After quitting the cattle business in Imperial Valley, he worked out of Los Angeles, buying cattle for the Cudahy Packing Company. He has since bought and sold cattle for himself, cut out beef for the California Cattleman's Association, bought cattle for the Alta Packing Plant at Munson, California, and done some cattle loan appraisal work for the Bank of America. The last time I heard from him, he was still living in his little cabin near the old Alta Packing plant at Munson, not far from Sultana.

———◆•◆———

MESA GRANDE CATTLEMEN

OTHER CATTLEMEN who at times wintered their stock in Borrego Valley were the Angel brothers and Arthur Stone of Mesa Grande in San Diego County. These men brought their cattle into Borrego by way of the old Hellhole Indian Trail, and their camp was on Palm Creek at the north boundary of the Park Headquarters Camp Ground. The desert willows at the edge of the creek bed where they had their open camp still stand with some of the overhanging limbs having been sawed off to make more room to move around in camp, and to prepare places to hang pots and pans. These men depended mainly upon the Palm Creek water for their cattle, and the length of time the water ran in the springtime ruled the length of time they could stay on the desert.

One winter when I was staying at the Frank Clark camp in the Valley, I would sometimes leave camp in the evening to take a ride among the cattle, stay wherever night overtook me, and then finish my ride very early in the morning when on my way back to camp to start the pump going to fill up the tank and watering trough. One evening I decided to stay at the Mesa Grande Boys' Camp for the night and visit with the Indian cowboy who was staying there. While visiting and talking over the more serious side of life, he told me that he wanted to ask me a question, and this is what he said: "Lester! I want to ask you a question. When you have been married by a Catholic Priest, and there was no marriage license, do you have to get a divorce before you can get married again? I have asked a great many people this question, but they give me different answers." I told him that I was unable to answer his question, for I was not experienced in getting married. He then said: "The reason I ask is this: There is another woman who is very much stuck on me; but, I am not very much stuck on her! She has a little money; not very much; about twelve hundred dollars; that is what I am stuck on!" Of course, we then discussed this very important and serious situation in general, but I never did learn anything about the outcome.

When I rode over the old Hellhole Indian Trail on my little mule a few winters ago, there was still evidence of how the Mesa Grande cattle would take shortcuts at the switchbacks in the old trail. However, the old trail is seldom used any more and perhaps the time will come when it will be very difficult to follow by an inexperienced person. I would like to see such old Indian Trails maintained and kept so they could be followed by hikers and horsemen. I do not mean by the use of machinery, but to be worked with hand tools to clear out the small stones and keep the way plainly visible.

PAUL AND PETE SENTENAC

PAUL SENTENAC and his brother, Pete, were old-time settlers at Sentenac Cienega, situated at the lower end of San Felipe Valley near where California Highway 78 enters the Anza-Borrego State Park from the west. Remains of the old Sentenac house can still be seen on top of a little hill to the right of the highway when starting down Sentenac Canyon.

A short distance across the Cienega to the southeast of the site of the old house can still be seen the remains of the old Sen-

The Paul Sentenac cabin at Yaqui Well, near the present Tamarisk Grove and Campground. (Howard Bailey collection)

tenac cattle corral. In 1910, when Tripp Brothers were driving about 280 cattle from the San Jacinto Mountain area to Imperial Valley, we put them in the old corral to hold them overnight. The upper side of the corral was made of stone, and the lower side was made of mesquite posts and poles. We did a foolish thing that night by making our camp just below the corral and tying our horses to the corral fence. Along in the night the cattle became frightened at something and ran into the fence where we had the horses tied and just above our camp. Fortunately, they did not hit the fence hard enough to break it completely down and come on over the top of our horses on us.

Enough of the fence posts were broken that the fence was leaning badly, and had that many frightened cattle piled on over the fence, it would have summed up to a very serious situation for horses, men, chuck-wagon and camp equipment. Many times since that experience, I have thought of what might have happened and have since taken much better precautions under similar possibilities.

Pete Sentenac died during his and his brother Paul's operations of their ranch, so Paul continued on in the business of raising cattle. He did not sell his steers regularly, so at times some of them were of considerable age before being sold, much older than the usual span of life for a steer. In 1904, Judd Tripp bought the aged Sentenac steers, but resold them without trying to fatten them, so I do not know how the new owner came out with them. My brothers, "Zeke", "Gib", and I bought some such old renegade steers one time and had very poor success in getting them fattened.

Paul Sentenac had a cabin at Yaqui Well that he used as a cattle-camp, of which there is a photo in these pages. The cabin has long since ceased to be, and the old well and cabin site are now a part of the Anza-Borrego State Park.

In later years George Sawday, a big cattle operator of San Diego County, became owner of the Sentenac property, and for many years Ralph Jasper who still lives on the old "Wid" Helm place at Montezuma Valley, leased the property from Sawday and pastured cattle there. The Jasper cattle grazed in Grapevine Canyon, Yaqui Well area, and during rainy seasons would range through the Narrows of the San Felipe Wash and get water from pools that would sometimes last for quite a period of time. The State Park Service now owns some of the Jasper property that came within the Park area, so the cattle no longer range in the vicinity of Yaqui Well. Cattle belonging to the Sawday interests now graze on the Sentenac Cienega.

When I went to the old "Wid" Helm place about two years ago to visit with Ralph Jasper, he told me that he had passed his 80th birthday, and I was pleased to see him still able to get around as he did. Should I live to that age, I hope to be able to get around as well.

When I was a very young boy, and "Wid" Helm still lived where Ralph Jasper now does, I heard cattlemen talk about the wild Helm steers that ranged in Upper Hellhole and other areas of the desert. They would talk about the Helm cattle ranging out to Fish Creek in the vicinity of where the Harper Well now is, and it was said that they sometimes would stray so far as to get across the Mexican Border. Those were the days when cowboys had to know how to live and survive under adverse situations and conditions.

CHAPTER 4

CATTLEMEN OF MASON VALLEY, VALLECITO
AND CARRIZO CREEK

RALPH BENTON of the Campo area and Archie Chillwell were early day cattlemen of the Vallecito Valley. I do not remember meeting Archie Chillwell, but I did meet Ralph Benton a few times when attending meetings of members of a cattleman's association.

Bert Moore and George McCain wintered cattle in Mason Valley, and of course Mr. Mason at times owned a small herd. I remember one time when I was very young, Ozro Tripp bought the Mason cattle, and wanted me to go with him to help gather and drive them to his ranch in the San Jacinto area, but I did not get to help him. I first met Bert Moore in 1910 when he was feeding cattle in Imperial Valley. George McCain I did not know so well as I did Bert Moore, but I first met him when he was associated with George Sawday in leasing the Warner Ranch.

Bob McCain cattle used the Canebrak Canyon area, and the Carrizo Creek area. When wet winters came on the desert, the Bob McCain cattle would range far out on the desert in the vicinity of Harper's Well and the Fish Creek Water. Some of these cattle were said to stay on the desert the year round. I first met Bob McCain in El Centro, the County Seat of Imperial County, when attending the trial of three men who were accused of butchering one of Bob's cattle.

HARPER BROTHERS

I CANNOT say what year I first met the Harper brothers, but it was at Temecula, when my father, brothers and I were shipping beef cattle, and the Harpers were there for the same purpose. I was greatly impressed with some of the fine Durham cattle in their herd. Julius D. and Amby H. were the names of the Harper brothers, and a son of Julius (E. Akim) now resides in Escondido.

In 1918 the Harper brothers and young Akim went into the Pinyon Mountain area to the east of the Blair Valley area to build dams—if I remember correctly two of them—in hopes of having a watering place for their cattle so as to use the feed in the flats to the east of the dams that still bear the Harper name. The dams were finished the winter of 1921-1922, but did not serve as a success, because of irregular and uncertain rainfall, and, too, because of the problem of sand filling up the space above the dams when sufficient rainfall did occur.

The old Harper Ranch is situated about 13 miles southeast of Julian, known as Harper Valley. About 1940, after the older Harpers had passed away, Akim sold the old ranch and he and the wife (Ethel E.) moved to Escondido in 1941 where they now reside. Early in 1962 I visited at the Harper home in Escondido where I enjoyed listening to him talk about the past in the cattle-world. Out in a shed back of the Harper home are numerous things to remind of days gone by, including his saddle with tapaderos on the stirrups, a rawhide riata, hair rope, chaps and spurs.

PROSPECTORS, GHOST MINE, AND BUTLER MOUNTAIN

TO FIND the Pegleg Mine, no doubt was foremost in the minds and hopes of all old-time prospectors in the Anza-Borrego area, including William Tripp, Sam Ferguson, the old colored man by the name of Howell, Dad Hardy, Howard Bailey, Bert Sommons, Charlie Carstesen, Charlie McVickers, "Old Man" Williams, Ozro Tripp and his son Chester. Of course, there were many others I did not know, but as a boy and young man, I knew all of those I have named, with the exception of the old colored fellow, Howell.

BUTLER MOUNTAIN

NOT SO very long after Samuel Tripp had bought the old Fain homestead, following Mr. Fain's death in 1883, from a gun shot wound in the head, a man appeared at the Radec Post Office where he introduced himself by the name of Butler. As I have stated at other times in these pages, the Radec Post Office was established by Samuel Tripp on the Fain homestead, and Mr. Tripp was the Postmaster. Somehow, Mr. Butler had learned that Will Tripp was the son of Samuel, and was very much interested in desert prospecting. After learning where Will Tripp lived, Butler asked to stay over night, and was permitted to camp in the ranch barn.

The following morning, Judd Tripp, one of Samuel's sons,

agreed to take a team of horses and a buggy, and go with Mr. Butler to Tripp Flats where Will lived. When Judd introduced Mr. Butler to Will Tripp, he related a story of having found a very rich placer gold deposit some years before when prospecting in the mountain bordering Borrego Valley to the northeast. After Mr. Butler finished relating his story of the rich placer gold deposit, Will agreed to give him a place to stay, and to grubstake him until the weather turned cool enough to make desert prospecting practical.

Mr. Butler appeared to be a very energetic man, and spent much of his time gathering crystal quartz to polish, and was free in talking about mining in general, so he enjoyed having a good place to stay and a generous supply of food. When the weather had cooled off enough so that Will Tripp thought the time had come when they should be going in search of the placer gold, a date was set to start on the venture. In the meantime, Will was busy getting the stock shod, and the camp equipment and food supply ready.

When the morning arrived for the start to the desert, the man Butler and his few belongings were nowhere to be found, so for the time the search for the placer gold was postponed. At the time, Frank Clark was carrying the mail from the Cahuilla Indian Reservation to the Radec Post Office, with team of horses and spring wagon. After Frank arrived at Radec with the mail, he met the man Butler in the orchard where he was eating a peach, and when Frank mentioned to Butler that he thought he was on the way to the desert, he ignored Frank's statement and said: "I'll declare! this is the most delicious peach I've ever tasted". The man Butler was not seen anymore by the Tripps, so whenever anything happened after that in the way of a failure pertaining to mining, it was referred to as another Butler, and Will Tripp started referring to the mountain bordering Borrego Valley on the northeast as Butler Mountain, and as a boy and young man, I knew of the mountain by no other name.

After Butler disappeared, Will Tripp and Sam Ferguson spent considerable time prospecting for the Butler placer gold, and for gold deposits in the vicinity of Old Borrego Spring, as had been described to Will by an old Indian lady when he taught school at the Cahuilla Indian Reservation.

The old Indian lady had told Will Tripp a story of how an Indian of the Cahuilla area would go to Old Borrego Spring to make camp, and after being gone from camp over night, would return with gold. In the Indian lady's story, she related that after Joe Marks established his store at Oak Grove where the old Butterfield Stage Station now stands beside California Highway 79, between Aguanga and Warner Hot Springs, the old Indian would trade his gold to Marks for groceries. However, Will Tripp and Sam Ferguson never did find the Butler placer nor the place where the Indian would get gold in the vicinity of Old Borrego Spring, so if these riches ever existed, the mystery of their where-abouts can still be a lure to present day prospectors.

In the winter of 1897 and '98, when the Tripps had their cow-camp in the lower part of Borrego Valley, the colored prospector (Howell) had his camp not far to the south, and of evenings they would visit to talk over the possibilities in prospecting on the desert. The old colored fellow enjoyed talking Mexican with Julio Montes, and in a tape recording Judd Tripp states the colored man could do a right good job speaking Spanish. The colored prospector had spent quite some time in the navy before he settled down on the desert in search of gold and other minerals.

"Dad" Hardy was one of the old-time prospectors who spoke often of Seventeen Palms, Old Borrego Spring, Palm Creek, Clark Lake, and Coyote Canyon. At times he would do the cooking at Clark Lake cow-camp, and I have seen him staying at Fred Clark's place at La Puerta when we would be gathering wild cattle. The last time I heard of anyone seeing "Dad" Hardy, was when Judd Tripp tells of seeing him at Modesto, California, about the month of August, 1917, when he was driving two burros to a small spring wagon.

Charlie Carstesen and Charlie McVickers usually did their prospecting together, and when not on prospecting trips they lived in the Temecula area. Charlie McVickers had a small place in the town of Temecula where he at one time ran a small restaurant and did bookkeeping for McSweeney Bros., who grew a large acreage of potatoes on the Vail Company's Great Pauba Ranch. Charlie Carstesen lived on a small place at the southeast corner of the Pauba Ranch beside California Highway 71 between the site of the old Radec Post Office and Temecula.

The two Charlies told of an experience they had one time in the finding of five human skeletons when traveling an old Indian trail between Old Borrego Spring and a point in the vicinity of Paloverde Wash. This old trail ran through the western edge of the Borrego Badlands, and at a later date Karl Bennis went with the two Charlies to see if they could again locate the five skeletons, but failed in their efforts, which was no doubt due to shifting sands and perhaps the effects of flood waters. They drove an old Hupmobile as near as possible to the place where the Charlies had seen the skeletons, and then made their search on foot. It was thought possible that the skeletons were of five men who had disappeared in

66

the desert a good many years before when on a prospecting trip and using good stock and equipment that old-timers thought may have been of interest to renegade persons, and the five men may have fallen victim to foul play.

I have heard desert men tell of another fellow who disappeared in the Borrego Badlands area. The story was that two men traveling with a light spring wagon or buggy camped at the Old Borrego Springs and one of them started on foot through the Badlands to meet the other one who drove the team and wagon to a point agreed upon for a meeting place. The man who was traveling on foot was never heard of again, and there were persons who thought he may have fallen victim to foul play through an old grudge concerning a hanging that took place outside California.

"Old Man" Williams, as he was called by those who knew him, usually traveled with burros pulling an old spring wagon, and would prowl around on the desert in the winter time, and then spend the summer time in the higher altitudes. The last time I ever saw the old fellow was one morning when I stopped at the Harper Well to water my saddlehorse and to get a drink of water for myself. I had camped out on the desert the night before with a damp saddle blanket over my shoulders and a bull terrier at my feet for a bed. I was trailing my brother, "Gib", who was following the tracks of three Arizona cows that had started back to Imperial Valley after being taken into Borrego with a herd a short time before.

When I rode up to the water at the well, Mr. Williams was camped there, and I asked if he had seen anything of a man riding a tall sorrel horse with white stocking legs. He said that he had seen him, and gave him his breakfast there that morning. Just as I mounted my horse and started to go, the old fellow asked if I had had any breakfast, and when I told him that Gib and I ate together in Borrego Valley very early the morning before and had not had anything to eat since, he swore as old desert men could, and in no uncertain terms announced that he was going to feed me, too. I put up no argument whatever, and the old fellow's "flapjacks" tasted about the best of any I have ever had the opportunity to appreciate and enjoy. Late that afternoon I caught up with "Gib" and soon after we found the three cows and put them inside a pasture fence. We found a place at the old Vendall Service Station where we could leave our hungry horses for the night with plenty of hay to eat, and caught a ride to Brawley.

"Old Man" Williams was a kind and honest man. My brother-in-law (Tom Whitlock) tells of loaning the old fellow ten dollars one time when he felt that he was just making him a present, but this old desert prospector was not happy until the ten dollars was paid back. I do not know what finally became of him, but hope that he was able to keep going until the very last, as I am quite sure was the hope of all the old-timers of the desert.

As late as about 1912, hopes of finding the Lost Pegleg Mine were running high in the minds of Ozro Tripp and his son, Chester, when they left San Jacinto, California with four horses hitched to a small wagon loaded with barrels for the hauling of water on the desert. Their destination was to some small black buttes or very rocky little desert hills to the north of the dry lake on Highway 78 where there are now two restaurants, each with a gas station, one of them bearing the name of Ocotillo Well, and the other Burro Bend.

Upon reaching their destination, Ozro and Chester joined with some other men who were working on what they had named the Three Buttes Mine. Chester Tripp being the youngest person in the group, was assigned the job of grazing the horses on Galleta Grass as they were taken each day to the Old Borrego Spring to be watered from the John McCain watering trough. The horses would then graze on the way back to camp where they were fed grain after being tied up for the night.

An attempt was made to develop a water supply by digging a well in low ground not far from the mine, but this was given up as a hopeless venture, and they went to some sand dunes to the southeast of the mine some little distance where the sand was damp on the surface, and there they dug a shallow hole in the damp sand, and by placing a barrel in the shallow hole obtained enough water to help in the supply for camp use.

The place then became known as Barrel Springs, but John McCain had known of the place for many years. John McCain had a name of his own for the place, but it was too unprintable for these pages. Howard Bailey and Bert Simmons would camp at this water when on some of their prospecting missions. A photo in these pages shows their camp equipment and the dishes being cleaned by the use of the fine sand of the surrounding dunes.

I do not remember how long the mining fever ran high at the Three Buttes Mine, but after work was suspended and the mine was more or less abandoned, wild stories began to get around about ghosts being seen in the vicinity of the mine. I heard one story that when someone had looked into the tunnel, a human skeleton was seen with a lantern burning inside it. Later on, I heard of an experience Bill Schnocka had when traveling in the vicinity of Barrel Spring and Three Buttes Mine.

Howard Bailey cleaning cooking utensils with fine sand at Barrel Spring. (Collection of Howard Bailey)

Bert Simmons flips a flapjack at Barrel Spring while on a prospecting trip with Howard Bailey in 1905.

Howard Bailey's wagon seems to be the better way to get around the Borrego Valley in 1910. He was hauling "tourists" from Warner's Hot Springs on a trip to the desert.

Howard Bailey and Bert Simmons on one of their prospecting trips in the Anza-Borrego desert.

Theodore Grand and Howard Bailey at the old Palm Spring (Mesquite Oasis) dugout. (Howard Bailey collection).

Theodore Grand and Howard Bailey at the old Palm Spring (Mesquite Oasis) dugout. (Howard Bailey collection).

Several times when with Bill, I failed to learn from him his story of the ghost, but one evening when we were riding after cattle in the vicinity of Tub Spring, and had been sitting on a little hill without any conversation passing between us, he started telling me the story of "His Ghost".

He told of starting to Brawley in Imperial Valley one late afternoon, after some heavy rains had fallen on the desert, thinking it a good time to make the trip while the sand was settled and making travel much easier for the two mules he drove to his wagon. He told of stopping some time after nightfall, when he was in the vicinity of the Three Buttes Mine and Barrel Spring, and unhitched the mules from the wagon, tied them to a wagon wheel to eat some hay he fed them.

After Bill had been asleep for a time, he was awakened by the mules snorting and jerking on the halter chains. When he sat up in his bed, he could see a moving light not so very far away, so he walked out toward the light to see if he could learn something about whether it was another desert traveler. However, when he would get near the light he could see it no more. He then went back to the mules and the wagon, and after a bit the mules had quieted down, so he thought he would let the mules eat a while longer and he could get some more rest before going on.

Not too long after getting to sleep again, he was awakened by the snorting of the mules, and this time they were really excited and indicating the possibility of getting loose and causing him to have to walk back home. He then decided the best plan was to get the mules hitched to the wagon and be on his way. Getting the mules hitched to the wagon he said proved to be quite a chore, but by holding onto the lines while getting the neck-yoke and tugs fastened, he was then able to keep them under control enough to scramble into the wagon. Bill stated that while he never had believed in ghosts, he was perfectly willing to let the mules set their own pace for awhile in getting away from the place, for he said he had to admit he was a bit bewildered, and could not imagine what the lights could have been.

While doing his shopping in Brawley the following evening, he made what he thought to be casual mention of his experience on the way to town, and returned to Borrego not thinking much more about the incident. However, when he returned to Brawley some time later, most everyone he knew wanted to know about "His Ghost".

As time went on, more stories were told about lights being seen in the vicinity of Three Buttes Mine and Barrel Spring, and it had become noticable that the lights were most likely to be seen soon after rains had fallen on the desert. Some of Bill's friends became so much concerned about trying to learn more about the mysterious lights, that they suggested a trip to the area to investigate.

Bill told of one man from the mountains who said that if he could get close enough to the lights, and they were the lights of a ghost, he felt quite sure he could get into conversation with it. When the investigating party arrived in the vicinity of the tunnel at Three Buttes Mine, Bill informed them that he was going to spread out his bedroll near an ironwood tree some little distance from the tunnel, but the rest of them wanted to be nearer the mine. Bill said that along in the night the gang came carrying their bed rolls down to where he was, and the man who was going to hold a conversation with the ghost said that when the light appeared, and he thought himself close enough to get into conversation, he found himself speechless. They made no further investigation, but returned to their homes, and when their experiences were related, officers of the law became interested and decided to make a trip to the scene of the mysterious lights.

The officers of the law were fortunate enough to have some of the lights appear, according to Bill's story, and they fired their guns at the spot where the lights were to establish markers and when close examination of the ground was made they found evidence of phosphorus, so they decided the lights that had caused so much excitement were phosphorescent lights. These findings ended the excitement and investigations, and Three Buttes Mine became known as "Ghost Mine".

Howard Bailey is the only one of the Anza-Borrego Desert prospectors whom I know is still living. As I have stated at another place in these pages he resides on the old Frank Clark homestead in Durazno Valley with his wife, Lola, who is the daughter of the late Frank Clark. Howard and Bert Simmons spent quite some time prospecting in the Anza-Borrego Desert area, using burros to ride and to pack. Howard's parents were some of the early settlers at Banner on Highway 78, between Julian and where Highway 78 enters the Anza-Borrego State Park. The Baileys owned mining property in Banner, including the old Ready Relief Mine.

Howard Bailey's and Bert Simmon's prospecting tours led them into the Fish Creek Mountain area where they worked their hyacinth mine. Howard tells of their digging into the sand in Fish Creek Wash above Split Mountain and getting water for themselves and the burros.

Howard Bailey tells of a time about 1906 when he and Bert Simmons were in the Borrego Area and planning a trip into Rockhouse Valley to do some prospecting. "Dad" Hardy at the time was staying with Fred Clark at La Puerta (San Carlos Pass), and somehow he heard of the planned trip to Rockhouse, so he sent word to Howard and Bert that he would like to talk to them before they went. With their burros, pack and riding animals, they went to the Fred Clark place by way of Coyote Canyon to see what Hardy wanted to talk with them about.

Upon contact with "Dad" Hardy, he told of having come through Rockhouse a short time before when he found two horses tied up without food or water, so he turned them loose. After waiting around a day or two, no one showed up to attend to the horses, so Hardy had left the horses loose and went on out to La Puerta.

Wondering what the situation in Rockhouse might be, Howard and Bert went from the Fred Clark place to their home in Oak Grove and started making preparations for the trip into Rockhouse Valley. They traveled by way of Lost Valley, following the old Indian trail that leads into the mouth of Alder Canyon, Fig Tree (Upper Willows), and to Middle Willows where they camped overnight. From Middle Willows, they traveled the trail across the mountain to the east, then by way of Hidden Spring, and on into the lower end of Rockhouse Valley where they made camp in the sandwash not far from a lone cottonwood tree where there was water.

After getting the animals unpacked and unsaddled, it was Howard's job to gather wood for a fire, and Bert would be the cook. Bert thought while Howard was getting the wood, he would take a look at the water. Soon he came hurrying back to camp, and excitedly told Howard of finding a dead horse lying partly in the water. They both went back to look the situation over, and found a pan for washing out gold and a canteen with new covering, each with a bullet hole made in them. Upon a little mesa above the water, they found a new pair of overalls and a blue shirt that had been torn into shreds, a blanket with blood on it, and off to one side at an ocotillo bush were the cooking utensils that had been left without being washed, and a bed roll with the name Archie Priest on it.

The following day when they were prowling around near a spring of water, and Bert was washing out some dirt to see if he could see any gold, Howard looked up on the side of the hill, and there stood an old Indian with a 30-30 rifle on his shoulder and carrying a forked stick in the other hand. They walked up the hill to where the old fellow stood, and could see that the rifle had some silver work on the stock, and took for granted the forked stick was used as a rest for the rifle when he wanted to shoot.

After talking with the old fellow for awhile, they invited him to their camp and asked him to eat with them. The Indian accepted the invitation, but would not take any of the food until he had seen them eat some of it. All the time they were eating the old man was talking about there being lots of gold quite some distance to the south, so they interpreted this as being a nice way of telling them they were not wanted in Rockhouse Valley.

They saddled and packed their animals the following morning and started over the old trail leading toward the east across the rugged mountains and into Martinez Canyon. After getting over on to the desert to the east of the Santa Rosas, riding their burros, they went to Indio to make inquiry and see if they could learn anything about what may have happened in Rockhouse Valley. At Indio, they learned nothing that would serve as a lead but when they arrived at Mecca, and made inquiry at a pool hall, they were informed that two men had walked out of Rockhouse saying their horses had been poisoned, and had then taken a train for Imperial Valley: Howard and Bert were then faced with a long trek back home with the burros.

The last prospector I saw with a burro pack animal, and he was traveling on foot, came to our camp at Clark Lake in the 1920's. He was a fairly old man who said he was from Pasadena, and that he was in search of a lost mine. The following morning he went across Clark Lake to Butler Mountain, and when evening came he was back at our camp very weary and saying he had searched out the Butler Mountain and was convinced the lost mine was not there, and stated that he had to go back to Pasadena to get his bearings and start all over again in his search for the lost mine. We did not see the old fellow again.

The same winter the prospector came to our camp, we saw our first airplane land in the Anza-Borrego Desert area. The plane came in, and after circling our camp a time or two, landed out on the smooth lake bottom. Through curiosity, we got into the Model T Ford and drove out to the plane. The first thing the pilot asked for was some baling wire. We had to laugh, because we had wondered at times when using baling wire to patch something, if it was ever used to patch airplanes.

CHAPTER 5

THE OLD POLE LINE ROAD, AND
LITTLE BORREGO TOWNSITE

DURING THE 1920's, the old-timers of the Anza-Borrego Desert and their era were due for a place in the history of the past. The present road had been built down Sentenac Canyon, a power line was running from Warner Ranch through a portion of the Anza-Borrego Desert to Imperial Valley, and parallel to a portion of the power line was what had become known as the Pole Line Road by way of Little Borrego—a desert townsite to the south of the present Burro Bend on Highway 78. Little Borrego, developed under what may be referred to as a booming atmosphere did not remain on the maps so very long, but right near by today, is a beautiful alfalfa ranch.

Cattle herds that were being moved between Imperial Valley and such points as Warner Ranch, Temecula, and San Jacinto mountain areas, were then being driven by way of Sentenac Canyon, the Narrows, Pole Line Road, Little Borrego, the County Well, then Harper's Well, and to Kane Spring on Highway 99, where the cattle were moved without road to follow, but keeping parallel to 99 until coming to the first irrigation canal. At that time, for the cook with the desert cattle drives, the automobile or light truck had taken the place of the team of horses or mules pulling the old style chuck-wagon.

Near Little Borrego townsite, we would pay for the privilege of watering the cattle at a newly developed ranch, where the owner would pump water into a trough for us, and because of limited watering space, we would be very busy for the greater part, if not all of a day or night getting a sizable herd of cattle properly watered, depending of course as to whether it was morning or evening when we arrived to water the cattle. The five day week, and the eight hour law, would have been misfits in such operations.

To water a sizable herd successfully at this place, required the help of about eight men. There would be the main herd to hold back away from the water quite some distance, those that had been watered, which of course would be building up all the while in number, and being anxious to graze after being watered would keep the cowboys busy. It was always necessary to have at least two men taking the small bands from the main herd to the water. The man who pumped the water for us was a fine fellow with whom to do business.

In the fall of 1925, my brothers "Gib" and "Zeke" and I were driving a herd of cows and calves to the Imperial Valley from our old ranches in the foothills of the San Jacinto Mountains. The route of travel of course was to be by way of Warner Ranch, San Felipe Ranch, through the Sentenac Canyon, and after leaving the San Felipe wash below the Narrows, we were to follow the Pole Line Road to Little Borrego where arrangements had been made to water the cattle.

After the cattle had been well watered and rested near Little Borrego, we were moving the cattle again, intending to take a short cut to the Fish Creek Water and Harper Well, after passing the County well. Some men who had driven a herd of cattle over the route some time before advised taking the shortcut saying that it would save us time and distance to the water.

After turning the herd on the advised shortcut, the lead cattle arrived at the Fish Creek water about ten o'clock in the forenoon. Immediately after arrival at the water with the lead cattle, my brothers "Gib" and "Zeke", began to realize what a mistake we had made by taking the shortcut, because it had led us to where the quicksand was bad, and some of the cattle were getting bogged so as to be unable to get out. They got very busy in getting the cattle away from this place and taking them to the spot on the creek where we had always watered before, and sent Francis McCarrol— an old Utah and Colorado cowboy—to meet me where I was making slow progress with the drags. The drags—with the exception of a few lazy ones—are the poorer and weaker cattle in a herd, and we would have had some losses had they not sent Francis McCarrol back to warn me of the situation. I followed the old route we had used on drives before, and arrived at our old watering place about half a mile or so to the north of Harper's Well where the main herd was being held while some of the boys were busy pulling cows from the quicksand. I well remember that my brother "Zeke" and "Red" Mitchell were taking the brunt of the work in getting the cows out of the bog.

The operation of pulling the cows from the quicksand lasted from 10 a.m. until it became too dark to work without endangering the saddlehorse to the quicksand. In addition to endangering the horse, the men who had been struggling in the quicksand for so many hours were due some badly needed rest and something to eat. The cook (Paul Kemp) had set up his cowboy's kitchen at Harper's Well.

Fortunately, the quicksand was not deep enough to cause an animal to sink out of sight, so the three cows we had to leave in the mire over night were not much more difficult to pull out than were those of the evening before, and all three of them were able to get to their feet and walk to the herd as had all the rest of the mired cattle. Some people say there is no such thing as luck, but if there is, he or she was certainly with us that time, when we had no losses of either cows or calves.

When we were on our way again with the cattle and driving just off Highway 99 a quarter mile or a little better, but traveling parallel to it, my nephew Harry ("Buck") Davidson when riding righthand point found a fair sized sandstone that had an imprint on the surface that certainly resembled the bare footprint of a human. He marked the place so that it could be found again and sometime later my brother "Gib" and Karl Bennis returned to the place and turned the stone over so that it would not be noticeable to anyone else that might be passing by. Karl Bennis returned again, and after chipping away a portion of the stone so as to lighten it, he managed to load it into his car, and the stone is now at Karl's place near Temecula, California.

The day following the finding the sandstone with the likeness of the bare-footprint of a human, the cattle drives came to an end soon after crossing the Trifolium Canal on Highway 99. The cattle were turned into a cornstalk field where they were rested for a few days before going on to better pasture.

The water I refer to as Fish Creek came by the name from a small blunt nosed fish in this stream, and as a young man I never heard the stream referred to by any other name.

Harper's Well during the many years the place has been familiar to me has been a well with a concrete top where water can be dipped through an opening in the cover which evidently was made for that purpose. A small stream of water flows from the well through a small opening in the side of the cover just below the larger opening of the top. Howard Bailey who is one of the more familiar persons with the Anza-Borrego Desert relates that the Harper's Well gets the name from the man who developed it, and tells of the materials for the building of the well and other operations being hauled with wagon and mule-team from Foster, in San Diego County. The well was developed in the 1890's, but Howard is unable to give the exact date.

At that time, materials from Foster to the Fish Creek area were hauled by way of Julian, Banner, San Felipe Valley, and from Sentenac Cienega over the hill to the east, then down Plum Canyon into the San Felipe Wash and follow the wash to make connections with the old wagon road leading into the Fish Creek area from Old-Borrego Spring and the site of the John McCain cabin. Another route was to go through Warner Ranch, then down Grapevine Canyon to the San Felipe Wash at a point near Yaqui Well and then follow the same route as taken after coming by way of Julian, Banner, San Felipe Valley, Sentenac Cienega, and Plum Canyon.

One cattle drive we made by way of Harper's Well and Fish Creek was with a herd of cows we moved from Imperial Valley to Borrego Valley when the rains came early and the flowers on the desert were at their best. These cows were bought in Arizona by Fred Palmer who now resides in Calipatria, and had the camera fans of today seen these cows growing fat and sleek from grazing on desert flowers, we perhaps would have heard from them in no uncertain terms; especially, had the owner of the house in which I am doing my writing—Ann Wissler—been among those camera fans. When I dare, I still remind her of what wonderful feed the desert flowers are for the cattleman's cows.

The first night out from the pastures of Imperial Valley, we made dry camp just after crossing the Trifolium Canal, intending to night-herd the cows until the break of a new day. Not too long after we thought everything was quiet for the night, something frightened the cows causing them to stampede. The moon was shining brightly, and having plenty of desert space, the cattle were circled, and after a time brought to a standstill—or rather to a halt under very nervous tension and milling around. They were then moved back to where they were being held, but in a very short time they were on the run again, and this time one of the cows broke a hip when they piled off over a steep bank, so we decided to keep them on the move toward Borrego.

Along in the latter part of the night, when we arrived near Harper's Well, another attempt was made to hold them until daylight. A very short time after most of the cattle were lying down and everything was perfectly still and quiet, they jumped to their feet as one—in the way that stampeding cattle do—and were on the run again. I was driving a model T Ford as chuck-wagon and had gone on up the road quite some distance to wait and see what happened. For this cattle drive we had hired a young Mexican who had not been out of Mexico but a very short time so we knew nothing of his experience, only what he told us. During this run, about twelve head of the cows broke away from the main herd with the young Mexican doing his best to keep them circling, and fortunately when he got them stopped, he was near enough to where I was waiting in the Ford, that I made him understand to hold them as near as possible to where he was for he was near the road where the other boys would be along with the main herd if luck stayed with them. It was not long until we could hear the other men coming with the main herd, and when the twelve heard the other cattle they were not too difficult to hold

The young Mexican cowboy was riding one of the three fillies we raised from the little mare that became victim of the bite of the sidewinder when on the cattle-drive by way of Carrizo Creek in 1910. As long as I live, I will remember my anxiety that bright moonlight night on the desert while listening to the patter of the hooves of twelve cows and the little mare when the young cowboy from Old Mexico was making such an earnest effort to keep the little bunch of cows circling in the vicinity of where the other men were having their troubles with the main herd.

The men did not stop the cows again until sometime after sunup when they decided the time for breakfast and the horses to have their grain was long overdue. While half the cowboys went to the chuck-wagon for breakfast, the other half stuck with the cows, circling around them all the while making a noise—singing we called it—so that the situation would not become too quiet, for that is the time when some sudden noise, such as a horse shaking himself, or at night when everything is very quiet the sudden lighting of a match will give them a perfect excuse to run. I do not know of anything that can occur more simultaneously than the way every animal lying down can be on his feet and on the run.

Not too long after the cowboys all had their breakfast, and the hungry horses enjoyed their grain and some rest, we again had the cows on the move toward Borrego, and drove them all day, with the exception of a few short stops to give them a little rest, which we begrudged them after they had been so determined to run. By evening they were beginning to be a fairly docile herd of cattle, and just before night we moved them away from the wash some distance below Old Borrego Spring and stopped them beside a steep bluff we hoped would help to hold them for the night. At this spot we were a little afraid that the hoot of an owl might frighten them, but we thought it best to take a chance, taking all other angles of the situation into consideration.

The cowboys, with the cook added to their numbers, split the hours of the night into guard shifts, with half the number standing guard at a time while the other half enjoyed some much needed sleep and rest. This night passed uneventfully, and the following day, the cowboys took a shortcut after watering their horses at Old Borrego Spring, while I went around by Frenche's Well with the Model T Ford chuck-wagon to meet them at the Clark Cattle Camp in Borrego Valley. This was the destination, and if ever we saw a docile herd of cows that had been so ready to stampede at the beginning of a drive, those old cows would have taken first place.

By the time we had arrived at our destination, we knew without doubt, we had made a good deal when hiring the young Mexican cowboy, and after the cows ran the first time, I remembered that the cows had stampeded the night before we loaded them at Pinto, Arizona, and three cows were killed by a passing train when some of them got onto the railroad right-of-way.

A short time after taking the Palmer cows to Borrego, we drove a small band of weaner calves belonging to Palmer over the same route to Borrego Valley, and this trip was uneventful until about half way between the dry lake where Burro Bend and Ocotillo Well are now situated beside Highway 78 and the Old Borrego Spring. I was again driving the Model T Ford chuck-wagon and it completely quit on me so I walked along behind the cattle until we arrived at the Clark Cattle Camp.

Quite some time before the two cattle drives from Imperial Valley into Borrego, and just after the heavy rains had fallen to make the desert flowers and weeds so good for the cattle, I made a scouting trip into the Anza-Borrego Desert with a Model T Ford stripped down so that just about all there was left were the parts necessary to keep it possible for the vehicle to run. When I stopped in at the hotel in Little Borrego intending to go on to Brawley, I was informed that the road between the County Well and Kane Spring was in a very bad condition due to the recent rains. I learned there were several men going to try to get through the following day, so I decided to stay over with them in their venture.

The following morning, twenty-one men gathered at the hotel with six cars, not counting the stripped Ford. They had plenty of rope for towing purposes, and were carrying shovels, so it was thought that that number of men should be able to get through with the cars. The first few washes we came to were not so very wide, and with twenty of us on the ropes and one man steering the car, the task of getting across was not too great. However, as time went on we were getting tired, our enthusiasm was beginning to fail us, and the washes were much wider than those in the first part of our venture. Eventually, we came to a very wide wash with banks several feet high, and very steep making a lot of shoveling necessary to get down into the mucky mess of mud and debris on the wide bottom.

We sized the situation up, including the steep bank on the opposite side, and when someone suggested we give up the idea, I well remember that I could think of no argument. During our struggle I had noticed a tall, quiet man from Texas who had very little to say, but was very willing to do his share of whatever there was to be done. When most of us started to walk back to Little Borrego, I noticed the man from Texas had not joined us. Upon arrival at the hotel, there sat the Texan at the wheel of his small Dodge truck. The Texan had worked his way between two of the washes until he was out of the main drainage, and then worked his way around on higher and drier ground until arriving at the hotel.

When those of us who stayed at Little Borrego had finished our breakfast the following morning, there was the man from Texas waiting with his Dodge truck ready to take us back to get the cars that had been left where we gave up the idea of getting through to Brawley. There were eleven of us then instead of the twenty-one that had gathered at the same spot the morning before.

We had traveled but a few miles when three head of cattle could be seen grazing not too far to the east of our route of travel. A rather noisy occupant of the truck asked the driver to stop, and when he stepped down from the truck and began talking about killing one of the cattle, it was amazing to note how readily six more of us were on the ground with the noisy individual and starting toward the cattle.

After moving toward the cattle for a short time, someone remembered that my 30-30 rifle was on the stripped Ford where it had been left the day before, and decided that it would serve much better for the killing of an animal out on the open range, than would the revolver worn by one of the men in the group. When everyone was back on the truck still talking about killing one of the cattle with my rifle, the driver started on his way again to where the other cars had been left the day before.

Soon after arrival at the cars, someone wanted to borrow a pocket knife, so when I loaned him mine he noticed how sharp it was and the talk started that it was the knife to use in the skinning of the beef. Taking into consideration that my rifle and my knife were to be used in the illegal killing of a beef, I decided that perhaps I had better start speaking my little part concerning the situation, rather than to wait until we got back to where the cattle were.

I started with what I had to say, by stating I had listened to a lot of talk about killing the animals, and that none of them knew but what my business in the area was to check up on such situations. Just then the man wearing the gun and badge stepped up behind me, and not having any way of knowing what his intentions might be, I turned facing him, feeling the most alone of any time during my entire life.

Up until then, the tall, quiet, soft spoken man from Texas had said not a word, and no one will ever realize how relieved I felt when he stepped out beside me and announced that he was with me in this situation. In his quiet manner, he then had considerable to say about our not having a right to kill one of the cattle without the owner's consent, and soon the situation was quieted down to where I thought I would have some more to say. I told them that if they felt the beef was really needed for food, I would put up ten dollars toward raising enough money to pay the owner for the animal, and wanted to ask that the money be turned over to the man from Texas, with the understanding he would see the owner received his money, and that I could tell them the owner of the animal as soon as I could see the brand, and would take upon myself the responsibility of the animal being butchered. They did not wish to accept this idea, so it was decided that we not kill the animal—at least not on the way back to Little Borrego.

After this incident occurred in the vicinity of Little Borrego, I had the opportunity to become fairly well acquainted with the tall quiet man from Texas. I found him to be a religious man, whom I thought of as coming much nearer to LIVING Christian Religion than do many of us. One time when getting my car stalled in a desert stream during a heavy storm, I walked to his place to get him to tow me out of the water, and then spent the night with him and his family. During our visit that evening we discussed the incident concerning the plan to kill the beef on the desert that time, and I reminded him that he never would know how relieved I was when he stepped out with me and announced that he was with me in the situation. He answered by stating that I never would know how happy he was when I gave him the opportunity to take a stand with me.

When we had to leave the stalled Model T Ford chuck-wagon in the wash to the south of Old-Borrego Spring, due to being very busy getting the new cattle settled in Borrego Valley, quite some time elapsed before my brother, "Gib", and I found time to return to the Ford to tow it to camp. Upon arrival at the place where we had left our chuck-wagon, it had very recently been towed away. However, to follow the tracks was like trailing an elephant in the snow, so it was not at all difficult to follow to where the Ford was sitting in a homesteader's yard, and the man and wife were nearby pumping up a tire for their car. The man was none other than the one who had been the most loud and noisy about wanting to kill one of the three cattle when we were on the way after the cars we had left behind when making the attempt to get to Brawley during flood times.

When we looked under the hood of the Ford, just about everything of any value had been stripped from it, and when I walked over to where the man was pumping up a tire with the hand pump, and asked if he would give us what had been taken from the Ford, he loudly announced: "There is your Ford just as I found it, so thought I had better tow it to my place before someone took the rest of it".

By this time I was really guessing what to do next, so I walked over to where my brother stood leaning against the man's car thinking to talk the situation over with him. Just then we noticed there was a quilt covering something that had been placed on the floor of the car between the two seats, so decided it would not cost anything to look underneath the quilt. I cannot say we were surprised to see the parts that had been taken from our Ford. I then walked back to where the man was working on his tire to talk about what to do concerning the situation. We decided that my brother and I would take the parts, let the matter drop, and tow the Ford to camp.

A few days later, when I stopped at Little Borrego on my way to Brawley to return Fred Palmer's Model A Ford to him which we had borrowed after ours had quit on us, I was approached by a man who lived not too far away, and he demanded to know if we were going to let the man get away with taking and stripping our Ford without doing anything about it. When I informed him that was our decision, he really told me what he thought about it, and stated we were just as bad as the one who took the Ford if we let the matter drop, for they had been wanting to get a case against the man for a long while, and they did not want to lose the opportunity that had now been afforded.

When I explained to the man that we were too busy to spend any time on the matter after getting everything back, and besides I was on my way to Brawley to deliver the borrowed car, he insisted that he follow me to Brawley to bring me back, and said he would take me to get the necessary papers sworn out, and stated that he would pay all necessary expenses. When I arrived in Brawley the man was right behind me, so we were soon on the way to Julian to learn what we had to do and where to go to have the papers prepared for the arrest of the man who had stripped the Ford.

When we arrived in Julian we proceeded to hunt up the constable, and he informed us we would have to go to Ramona to get the warrant made out. By that time it was after night, and knowing we could not get to Ramona in time to find the Justice of the Peace at his office, we decided to stay at a hotel in Julian. When time came to pay the hotel bill and to pay for our meals and gasoline, the man who had insisted upon getting out a warrant said that he was not carrying any money with him, so if I would take care of the expenses he would settle up with me when we returned from the trip.

Upon arrival in Ramona, we were informed the Justice was serving on the bench in San Diego for the month, so we were on the way to San Diego—the man just had to be arrested. The man who insisted upon the arrest being made then took me back to Borrego. Some time later, my brother and I were notified of the date for the hearing in San Diego.

When we arrived at the court house in San Diego, and before court was called to order, the justice called my brother and me out into the hall and asked just how serious we felt the case to be. We related the story to him, and stated how we had not wanted to make any arrest because of having the Ford parts back, and emphasized the fact that we were very busy with the duty of taking care of the cattle.

When court was called to order, and my brother and I were called to the witness stand, there sat the wife of the man who had stripped the Ford, in the front row with several children—perhaps some of them borrowed. My brother and I were not questioned for very long, and then released to get back to our duties. I never did learn the outcome of the trial, but the man was back on the desert immediately after trial, and the neighbor who insisted upon his arrest is still "going" to pay the expenses of bringing into being the necessary papers.

The last time I was with a herd of cattle over the Old Pole Line Road, was in September of 1932, when moving a herd of over four hundred cows with more than three hundred calves for the Vail Company. The cattle were started from Vail's Great Pauba Ranch at Temecula, and taken to their ranches in Imperial Valley.

We were on the road thirteen days and nights with this slow moving herd, and at no time in my life have I spent as much of the time when on a cattle drive without sleep, as I did this time. When we did have an opportunity to get some sleep, it was never for very long at a time.

At the present time, when cattle are moved over this route, it is all done with fast trucks that cover the distance in much less time than either a day or night. I enjoy thinking back over the incidents of the old cattle-drives, but do not feel badly when realizing there will be no more cattle-drives to Imperial Valley for me, even though this last summer of 1962 I helped move over six hundred in Tulare and Inyo Counties, a drive that required seven days, split into two sessions, one of three days, and of course the other of four days. Yes, the days of the cowboys and the cattle owners in the Anza-Borrego Desert now belong in the history of the past.

The old Terwilliger home at La Puerta, now known as Terwilliger Valley on the southeastern corner of Anza Valley. The elder Terwilligers on the right, their daughter Annie and her daughter Pearl on the left, and Francis Hopkins in the center. Annie was the wife of Frank Clark.

The Vallecito Stage Station in 1912, when Ozro Tripp, his son, Chester, and the author visited it. (Lester Reed collection)

CHAPTER 6

DESERT CATTLE DRIVE IN 1910

IN 1910, the Imperial Valley was becoming a great feeding ground for cattle, and many of them were being shipped or driven there to be fattened for the better prices of the winter market. This valley is situated in the southern end of California to the east of the Coast Mountain Range, and adjoins the Mexican Border in the Mexicali area.

On September 1 of that year, my father (Quitman Reed) and I started with a small herd of cattle to meet other cattle owners at the Warner Ranch, from where we intended to put the cattle into one herd to drive them across the desert to the pasture lands. The Warner Ranch at that time was operated by the Vail Company, grass conditions were excellent, so the cattle were well filled and rested before starting on the trek across the desert that was so hot and dry at that time of year. The cattle drive was to be over the old Butterfield Stage Route by way of Carrizo Creek, and this was to be the first time my father had been over the old route since traveling by ox-team with his parents in 1867. After traveling across the desert for a few days, he said that they must have had great hopes of something better on the other side to keep them struggling along over such long stretches of sand.

When we started the drive from Warner Ranch there were six hundred and thirteen cattle in the herd, belonging to several different owners. By putting our cattle together for the drive we were able to move them at a minimum of transportation cost. However, on such drives, some of the cattle would get so sore footed that quite some time was necessary for them to recuperate before starting to fatten for the market.

The first day out from Warner, we were on the San Felipe Ranch, where we first began to see signs of the desert, and near the lower end of the ranch we came to a barbed wire enclosure with a fine stream of water running through. Within this enclosure was where the cattle were held for the night, so everyone appreciated the fact there would be no guard duty during this night unless something happened that would frighten the cattle and cause them to stampede.

We left the enclosure very early the following morning, and after a few miles of traveling we were in terrain strictly of the desert, and the shrubbery consisted mainly of mesquite, catsclaw, desert "willow", ocotillo, mescal (agave), smoke tree (desert pine), soap brush, jumping cholla, and many other plants of the desert—in some places the juniper.

During the day, after leaving the San Felipe Valley, we then passed through Blair Valley, evidently a portion of it being a dry lakebed during the years of heavy rainfall down through the many centuries of time. A grove of mesquite trees was growing in what appeared to be the old lake bottom. From Blair Valley the cattle entered the historic Box Canyon that narrowed down to just the width of the old wagon road, and here the herd was strung out so that from the time the leaders entered the canyon until the drags came along, forty-five minutes time had elapsed. It is always pleasing to a cattle owner to see them strung out in this manner, for when they do, they are traveling with a minimum of wear on their feet.

The Box Canyon is a strip of the old Butterfield Stage Route mentioned previously in these pages, over which many of the homesteaders traveled during their rush to Imperial Valley to file claims on the lands that had been opened to entry under the newly developed irrigation system. Tom Whitlock, (my brother-in-law) now at the age of seventy-seven in 1962, traveled through the canyon with teams and wagons in 1902, and he tells about the longer vehicles—such as the long feed-racks used on farms for the feeding of the farm teams—being much too long for the crooked, narrow road winding down the bottom of Box Canyon. On the sharper turns, the hind wheels of the longer vehicles would not be following the tracks of the front ones, so the walls of the canyon would keep shoving the rear ends back into place.

After passing through the canyon with the herd of cattle, we entered into Mason Valley, named for an early-day homesteader. The homestead buildings at that time were four in number, all being rather small, and the living quarters were built of adobe. Not too far from the Mason buildings, the road led from the valley over a very rocky hill where the way was narrowed down again

Box Canyon in 1912. It was a very narrow road, part of the Butterfield Stage Route. (Photo by Edith Tripp Reed)

Olin Bailey homestead near Vallecito Stage Station in 1910. (Howard Bailey collection)

The Mason homestead in Mason Valley, in 1912. The four buildings were constructed of adobe. (Lester Reed collection)

to the width of the wagons and the same length of time passed for the herd to pass through as was the case at Box Canyon.

The old road down the east slope of the Mason Hill was very steep, and Tom Whitlock tells of homesteaders' vehicles being wrecked on one of the worst turns because of brakes being inadequate to hold on such steep, rough roads. Evidence of such wrecks remained for quite some time along the road down this hill, but at this writing evidence of the wreckage has all disappeared, perhaps by way of souvenir hunters, gathering firewood, and metal parts taken for scrap. During this rush of people to the Imperial Valley, some vehicles were abandoned long before reaching the rough spots on the desert, for I remember seeing some of them along the way of steep narrow roads that wound through the hills south of Hemet.

After passing over the rough road down Mason Hill, we turned the cattle off the road to the left, to hold them for the night on the small stream of water running through the narrow canyon leading from the lower end of Mason Valley. On this small stream of water the cattle became very restless, and soon the water was so muddy the cattle would not drink as we had hoped, and they became very difficult to hold. In addition to the cattle being restless because of watering conditions, the jumping cholla was plentiful, and whenever one animal became victim to the cholla, they would start running and kicking, causing other cattle to get into the chollas, and then we would have quite a task keeping them under control. We learned the chollas burned freely, so we kept the canyon very well lighted, and by morning the cholla problem was very much reduced.

The following day was very hot, and even though we had the cattle on the way early in the morning, we made very little progress with the thirsty herd. During this day we passed to Old Vallecito Stage Station, where during the days of its occupation, two men were killed simultaneously in a shooting between the two over a poker game. In the story of this killing, as told to me by Judd Trip—an old-timer of the desert—the bodies of the victims to the shooting were buried in the little cemetery on the small hill to the east of the station, but after a time were moved to Julian. As the story of the shooting was told to me, the wives of the shooting victims walked from Vallecito to Julian to get away from the scene of such tragedy.

At Vallecito was an old-time roadside watering trough where we watered the saddle horses and the chuck-wagon team, but the herd of cattle of course could not be watered there. That evening the cook drove the chuck-wagon to Palm Spring (Mesquite oasis), another wayside watering place for saddle horses and work teams;

it was a good place for the cowboys to have the evening meal. About one half mile from the spring the herd was stopped with the intention of holding them there until early morning.

At this spring was another one of the old-time wooden watering troughs, and hanging near the end of the pipe that carried the small stream of water into the trough was a dipper made from a gourd, and on the bottom of it was written with pencil this verse:

"Here's to the girl I love
And I wish that she were nigh,
If drinking here would bring her near,
I'd drink this damn trough dry."

By the time every one had taken his turn to have the evening meal, the thirsty cattle had convinced us that they were going to be very difficult to hold for the night, so the decision was to try letting them drift down the wide sand wash to the water at Carrizo Creek, a distance of several miles. Two other young men and I were sent ahead to Carrizo Creek to get some rest before the lead cattle would arrive, and it would then be our job to hold the cattle on the water while those who followed in with the drags could have their turn at trying to get some sleep and rest.

When daylight came there were no cattle in sight, but from quite far away we could hear some of them bawling as thirsty cattle will. The three of us saddled our hungry horses and started on the way to meet the herd, and learned when we met the two men with the drags (my father and a young man by the name of Orval Kolb, that the lead cattle had turned up a side wash, and then headed back toward the water below Mason Valley. Quin Davidson and George Dameron had already turned back to start gathering the cattle they knew would be at the water. Just about half the herd had turned back. The two young men that were with me (Gilbert Miller and Henry Smith) turned back with the cattle that my father and young Kolb were driving, so my father, Orval Kolb and I started working back along the banks of the wash to look for tracks of any cattle that might not have gotten headed back to the water. I was working the east side of the wash, and had not traveled very far when I found where a small bunch had started up a wash toward the badlands, and this did not tend to make me feel at ease this time of year for I was not carrying any water with me.

Fortunately, the cattle did not follow the wash very far, for they had come to a low place in the ridge on the north side of the narrow wash, where they had crossed over and got headed in the right direction. I then kept to the east of their sign in order to watch for sign of others that might have wandered too far in the wrong direction. I did not find the tracks of any more cattle wandering to the east, so I worked my way back to near the road and main travelway where I met the cook (Mitt Dameron) with the chuck-wagon. The cook gave me a drink of water and handed to me a quart can of tomatoes and a small can of corned beef to carry back to where I would make contact with the other men gathering up the cattle.

Later in the day, quite some distance away, I saw my father ride to the top of a ridge, so I knew he was riding up there for a better view and was looking for me. He had seen me take up the side wash leading toward the badlands, so was wondering and getting anxious to know how much of a jaunt I might have had to take without water. I rode to the top of another ridge and waved my hat, and he immediately waved in answer. Even though quite some distance separated us, I could note his feeling of relief after he had seen me wave my hat. The drink of water he gave me from a canteen was quite welcome, but would have been much more so had I not met the cook with the chuck wagon.

My father and I were now at a point where it was no longer necessary to watch along the sides of the travelway for signs of straying cattle, so we started with the intention of going to meet the other three men who were gathering up the cattle so we could again have them headed in the direction of Carrizo Creek.

I do not remember just how many cattle we were short at the end of this day, but not so very many. At Caliente we stopped for the night where we repaired an old wire fence enclosure we hoped would keep the tired sorefooted cattle from straying away, for our poor horses by this time were sorely in need of food and rest. By taking chances on the enclosure holding the cattle, our horses got some rest, but there was no food for them at all. The five of us shared the can of tomatoes and the can of corned beef, and the summer weather and the sand wash had to serve as our beds, for our saddle blankets were too wet with sweat to be of any use to us.

The following morning we were on our way very early, for we were not "bothered" with the cooking of breakfast—not even with the making of coffee. This day was very hot, so progress with the cattle was slow through the middle of the day. We arrived at Carrizo about ten o'clock that night, where the cook and the two cowboys were having their troubles trying to hold their half of the herd. The cook was riding one of the chuck-wagon horses with a blind bridle and no saddle, and he was truly a busy man, for three men with that many restless cattle to try to hold day and night had summed up to a very sleepless session, although they did have food for themselves and their horses.

The five of us who went back to gather up the cattle that strayed away in search of water, were out two nights, two days, and until ten o'clock the third night with only the can of tomatoes and the can of corned beef to eat. I imagined that if I ever caught up with the chuck-wagon, I would be able to eat everything in it at one meal, but to my surprise, I could eat but very little the first meal. However, we all did justice to what the cook prepared for us the second meal. The poor horses were the ones that had really suffered while getting the straying cattle to Carrizo Creek, for there was nothing at all for them to eat, and we had to work them hard. The only opportunity we had to take the saddles off their backs for any length of time was the night at Caliente.

After the cook fed us at Carrizo that night, and our horses had time to eat for awhile, we gathered up the cattle the best we could and moved them to dry ground away from the water to be held until daylight. At one time when the cattle were quiet, I got off my horse to rest her and myself for awhile, and for the first time I had ever had this occur, the horse lay down with the saddle on and stretched out on her side to get some of the rest her weary body so badly needed.

When daylight came we moved the cattle back to the water where some of us were to hold them until about 10 A.M. while others scouted around to gather up what we had missed the night before. While holding the cattle at the water, a shepherd dog belonging to some people crossing the desert with team and wagon, brought in the greasy thigh bone of a human. This served as a "gentle" reminder of what can so easily happen to a person on the desert during the summertime.

Soon after ten o'clock in the forenoon, when we thought everything had been gathered, the cattle were started on the thirty mile trek to what was then the Westside Canal of the Imperial Valley Irrigation District. The plan was to slowly move the cattle as far as the weather would permit during the rest of the day, and then drive all night in order to arrive at the canal before the sun got too hot the following day. About two or three miles from the water, a fine whitefaced three-year-old steer, and a husky black cow began to stagger and walk in circles, then fell over and died in a very short time. We thought the death of these two cattle to be the result of the hot weather after getting too thirsty and drinking too much of the Carrizo Creek water, which I have often said tasted but little better than the treated water we humans find ourselves drinking today. Watching these two cattle die in such a manner, served as another reminder of what so easily can happen to humans under conditions causing them to drink too much poor water.

For quite some distance after leaving the water at Carrizo Creek, the old Butterfield Stage and Immigrant Route ran parallel to the Carrizo Wash, then turning more to the southeast, the road led up the Blue Hill, over which the cattle had a very steep climb. When coming down this steep hill, the vehicles of the covered-wagon trains often had to be what the old-timers called rough-locked in order to have sufficient brakes to hold back the heavy loads.

Not long after leaving the top of Blue Hill, we passed a grave just a short distance from the road and to our right. Judd Tripp told of the grave being that of an old Dutch fellow who had stopped at his place near Aguanga, on what is now Highway 79 to buy some hay for the two horses he was driving to a wagon. The old fellow was on his way to Imperial Valley where he had filed on a homestead claim. On the wagon the Dutchman was hauling his few belongings, including some ducks and geese, so Judd cautioned him about the hazards of crossing the desert in hot weather, and made special mention of the hot sun being rough on any kind of domestic fowl.

Judd had learned the old fellow had met with some other people at Carrizo Creek who wanted him to travel with them, for they thought they could save him some time as they were going to take a shortcut on the way to the canal. After following his escorts for some time, the old fellow decided they were lost, so he turned back. He found his way back to the main road all right, but when found by some other desert travelers he was in an unconscious state and there were indications that he had tried to save the ducks and geese by pouring the last of his water from the canteen into a little hole he had dug in the dirt. The people tried to revive him, but their efforts were in vain, so they buried him there, and marked the grave with stones. I went back to the spot about three years ago, but was unable to be sure that I found the grave.

When night came upon us at the end of this day out from Carrizo Creek, we were driving the cattle through a strip of sandy desert where the little rattlesnakes (the sidewinder) were very plentiful. About 9 P.M. I heard the fifth one of the little snakes making an excited noise as he came out from under my horse on the right side. This snake made the fifth one I had heard in about two hundred yards distance, and it was not long until my horse began to limp in the left front leg. When I ran my hand along her ankle, I could feel a small damp spot, and by the light of a match I could see the two tiny spots of blood where the fangs had entered. It is very likely she had stepped on the snake, and I had led her but a very short distance when she became so sick that she lay down and stretched out on her right side. Thinking it would be wrong to try to make her travel I took my saddle from her back, and from the way she appeared to be suffering, I thought she surely would die, so I started walking to overtake the cattle.

As I walked away from my horse thinking I was leaving her to die from the snake bite, my thoughts in general about the desert were not at all pleasant ones, I thought of the desert as a land of hot sun, a land where people perished because of the need for water, a land where horses and cattle suffered because of the long distances between water, a land of thorns and deep sand very difficult to travel over, and most certainly a land of sidewinders.

The time was eleven o'clock at night when I caught up with the cattle where the men had stopped them for a rest. My father unsaddled his horse to relieve his back while we tried to get some rest before going back to get my saddle. To our surprise the horse was still alive, but her entire body was terribly swollen, and she was in exactly the same position as I had left her. We had no gun with which to put her out of her misery, and we felt that we must not leave her there to die from heat and thirst. We decided to get my saddle tied so that it would ride upon the hips of my father's horse, and I then picked up a stick and rushed up to the sick horse making all the noise that I could, striking the ground with the stick thinking that perhaps she would be frightened enough to scramble to her feet. The effort was successful, and we immediately got her on the move feeling that we should not take a chance on letting her stop.

When we got back to the chuck-wagon, one of us transferred my saddle from the horse to the wagon while the other kept the sick horse on the move so that she would not lie down, for we had little hope we could frighten her enough to get her to her feet again.

We did not try to stay back with the cattle, but went on ahead taking turns at riding my father's horse, while the other walked holding on to the tail of my father's horse which was a great help over the soft sand. The one who was walking kept the victim of the snake bite traveling beside the other horse. As I have lived down through the years, I have seen very few horses that I believe could have been made to travel as this one did despite the horrifying condition she was in.

While my father and I were trying to get some rest before going back after my saddle, I had tied my hat to one of the stirrups of my father's saddle. My reason for tying my hat to the stirrup was to keep the strong wind from blowing it away, but at 1 A.M.

when we were ready to go after my saddle, the wind had thrashed my hat around so much that the string had worn out and the hat was gone. The following morning when the hot sun began to take over, I used as a hat the nosebag we were carrying to feed grain to the horses.

On our way to the water in the Westside Canal, we passed a tiny grave that was off the road to the right with a little cross we thought to be a marker for the head of the grave. We were afterward informed that the little grave was that of a young baby who died while the parents were traveling over this stretch of dry desert during the homesteader's rush to the valley. About three miles before getting to the canal, we passed another grave that was a short distance off the road to the left. This grave was that of a husky young man who failed to make it to the canal water when he was traveling on foot.

Judd Tripp again related the story of this young man's misfortune. The husky young man by the name of O'Brien had arrived at the Mason Homestead with no container of any kind for carrying water, and when Mr. Mason noticed this, he insisted on giving him a quart bottle, and cautioned him not to try to make the distance from Carrizo Creek to the canal in the day-time. We did not learn if the young man's failure was due to trying to make it in the daytime, but when his body was found about two weeks later, he evidently had tried to get relief from the shade of a bush.

We arrived at the canal about 9 A.M. with the victim of the snake bite, and the last of the cattle were to the water sometime before noon. The cattle were held under guard that night not far from the water, and the following day the drive came to an end when we turned the cattle into a stubble-field near New River, where they were to recuperate from the hardships of the desert before we separated them for the different owners to take to the green pastures of alfalfa and cornstalks. I had made arrangements with the caretaker of the canal (zanjero) to take care of my horse until we had the cattle placed as we wanted them.

About two weeks time passed while we were getting the cattle to the pastures where we wanted them. Some of these pastures were on the east side of the Imperial Valley near the town of Holtville, and one of these pastures was owned by Frank Powell, a member of one of the families of the wagon train with which my father had come from Texas in 1867, so he and my father had quite a lot in common to talk about.

When the cattle were all placed as we wanted them, I borrowed a two horse team and wagon from Bert and Arthur Tripp to go get my horse and haul her to the Tripp Ranch. Upon arrival at the zanjero's place, he told me that he was afraid my horse was going to have to give up her battle for life, because she had eaten but very little in the last several days. However, we dug holes in the ground so as to let the hind wheels down to where the rear end of the wagon bed came even with the surface of the ground. By putting ropes around the horse's very sore front ankles and pulling one foot forward at a time, we managed to get her to the rear of the wagon bed where by the same method we got her into the wagon. It was now after dark when I got on the way to the Tripp Ranch near Heber, a distance of about twenty miles.

During the night the sick horse would hold her head around by her side as if suffering severely from the effects of the snake bite and the jolting of the wagon over the rough and dusty dirt road. Her ears were very cold, and I could not help thinking of this as a bad sign, but I kept on my way, hoping for the best, and arrived at the ranch about four o'clock in the morning.

In making preparations for the unloading of the horse, I backed the wagon to a ditch bank where very little digging was necessary to lower the hind wheels so that the rear of the wagon bed was even with the surface of the ground. By again tying ropes around her front ankles and pulling her front feet backward one at a time she was unloaded from the wagon, and when she whinnied to me I thought of it as being a bit of encouragement.

Soon after the animal was unloaded from the wagon, a Mexican by the name of Frank Dostle came riding up on horseback, and he became very much interested and concerned about the condition of the entire body of the snake bite victim. Her skin was badly broken, and large pus pockets had formed in many places on her body and down to her hooves on both front legs. After Dostle had examined her thoroughly, he asked for permission to take over the job of trying to save her life. I could see that he was a man who truly appreciated animals—and especially horses—so he was given permission to take over her care. I told him to give me an order for whatever medicine he would need. He apparently knew without hesitation just what he wanted, and the horse became his patient.

Frank Dostle was working on a nearby ranch, but whenever he had a little spare time he could be found with his patient, and to this day, there is no doubt whatever in my mind that it was his care that saved the life of the victim of the bite of the sidewinder. For more than six weeks time she would not try to lie down for the rest she so badly needed, and this was due mainly to the condition of her front legs. When she did begin to venture lying down, we would have to make her get onto her feet again so that she would not suffer the effects of being in one position too long.

One day Dostle announced that she had gained to where green feed would be the best medicine she could have, so she was turned into an alfalfa pasture, and before long she began to resemble a horse again. During this process of recovery, both her front hooves grew off just as a thumb or finger nail does when hit with a hammer or injured in some other like manner.

The new hooves were so ill shaped that we never tried to use her again in working with cattle, but she raised us three fillies that broke out to become among the better cow-horses I have used. One of them—Marie—proved to be very difficult to ride when we first started to break her. One morning she threw me directly over her head, resulting in nine hundred and fifty pounds of horse and saddle landing on three feet between my shoulders. At times now, about fifty-two years later, I have trouble with what I call the horse tracks between my shoulders. Marie later became one of the best reined and well trained cow-horses I have ever known, after being trained by my brother, Albert ("Zeke") Reed.

Many times when working cattle on one of the fillies we raised from the victim of the bite of the sidewinder, I wondered what the difference might have been had my father or I either one been carrying a gun that night on the desert when we went back to get my saddle thinking that the little mare surely would be dead. Would we have shot her to put her out of her misery, or would we have given her a fighting chance? It sums up to a very serious situation when a man is faced with what appears to be the necessity of shooting his dog or horse.

We sometimes meet with persons who claim that the bite of a rattlesnake is not serious and I do not choose an argument, for I can only speak from my own personal experiences. While we were camped near New River in Imperial Valley the time my horse was victim to the snake bite, a white mule at camp was bitten on the end of the nose between the nostrils and the wound was treated by cutting with a razor blade to cause bleeding and the mule lived. However, his head became severely swollen.

At the same time, about half a mile from where we were camped a man running a fresno scraper in the leveling of land was bitten on the ankle and died from the effects. He may have been exercising strenuously at the time which would tend to rush the poison through his system.

About ten years later—on the first day of May—when helping move a small herd of cattle we had bought, the buckskin colored horse I was riding stepped on a large red rattlesnake and it bit him on the ankle. We were about half a mile from a homestead, so I went to the house and asked for some kerosene, stating that I wanted it to treat a snake bite on my horse's leg. The lady to whom I was talking announced that they had some permanganate of potash and a syringe with which to use it. The lady made a good assistant in doctoring the horse, for she was not at all afraid to hold his head while I injected three shots of the permanganate solution into the wound. We then bathed the wound with kerosene, and I went on home—a distance of about six miles—riding the horse and helping with the cattle, and the horse's leg became only slightly swollen.

Since experiencing the events of the cattle-drive through a portion of the Anza-Borrego Desert in 1910, I have traveled many miles and spent a lot of time in this desert area, and have learned to greatly appreciate all that it holds in the Story and Religion of The-Big-Outdoors. I have learned that the warm sunshine, the rain, and the deep sands can produce wonders in the growing of Mother Nature's Flower Garden. I have learned that the thorns serve to protect the plants from over-browsing by hungry animals, and as a refuge for God's smaller creatures when being pursued by the larger ones. Since growing older, I have come to believe that the Creator surely must have had a reason for placing the sidewinder on the desert, and I do know that some of the desert Indians will not kill them.

Frank Hamilton was a descendent of Indians who one time lived in San Felipe
Valley. He died in 1895 from wounds
received in a gun battle with Charlie
Marshal at San Jacinto.

Charlie Brown (Carlos Moreno) who
named Monkey Hill while camping with
the Clark Brothers. Charlie was an ex-
pert horseman and cowboy.

CHAPTER 7

COYOTE CANYON

THE UPPER end of Coyote Canyon begins at the confluence of Horse Canyon from the north; Nance Canyon in the center running mainly from a northwesterly direction; and Tule Canyon also converging from a northwesterly direction. Along the Coyote Canyon the trees and shrubs consist mainly of cottonwood, willows, mesquite, desert willow, desert pine (smoke tree), catsclaw, creosote bush, different varieties of cactus and cholla, and many other varieties.

The mountains on the east are very rugged, rough desert formations, very steep, but not so very high. Bordering on the west, the mountains at the base are of desert formations, but they extend to higher elevations than those on the east, they are covered with growth belonging more to the mountain areas.

The first water rising in Coyote Canyon as one travels down the Canyon from the north is what was known to the oldtime cattlemen as Fig Tree (Upper Willows). The second water rises at Middle Willows, which, fortunately, has retained the name the old-timers had for it. The third and last water rises in a valley of considerable acreage, known to the old-timers as the Joel Reed Valley. At the present time, through persons who came into the area about 1910, the Joel Reed Valley lost the old-timer's name to a family by the name of Collins.

The stream of water that runs from the Joel Reed Valley is said to be the largest stream of year-round running water in San Diego County, much of it coming from the Joel Reed Spring (Santa Caterina Spring).

At the upper end of Joel Reed Valley, not too far below Middle Willows, is a small rocky hill, apart from the hills on either side of the Valley. This hill still retains the name of Monkey Hill, so named by one of the old-time cowboys of Coyote Canyon and

Borrego Valley. The cowboy's name was Charlie Brown (Carlos Moreno) who had worked on the Warner Ranch before coming into the area. On the Warner Ranch is a hill by that name; and the hill in the upper end of Joel Reed Valley reminded Charlie of it, so he started calling it Monkey Hill, and I am very happy to know that the little hill has retained the old-timers' name for it. If Charlie were still alive, and mention of Collins Valley was to be made to him, he would wonder what place we were talking about. The same would be true with Will Tripp and Frank Hamilton who served as witnesses for Joel when he made proof on his claim.

The Monkey Hill on Warner Ranch is near enough to Henshaw Dam that it becomes an island when the water rises high enough to run over the dam, and when I was a small boy, I was told that this hill came by the name because of a monkey that lived there for a time after escaping from some gypsies. I do not know if this story is authentic or not, but I did know the Charlie Brown who named the Monkey Hill in the upper end of Joel Reed Valley.

Charlie Brown, when working in Coyote Canyon as a cowboy, always spoke of Coyote Canyon, Borrego Valley, and the Clark Lake as "The Ranch", and he called the Indian horses in the Coyote Canyon area the "The Ranch Remuda". When I was a small boy, Charlie called me Palomino (Palomillo) because of the color of my hair. Palomino (Palomillo) is what the Spanish or Mexicans call certain horses of light color.

A tributary to Coyote Canyon near the mouth, and converging from the east is the one the old-timers called North Canyon, but now has the name of Box Canyon. Beginning at the upper end of Coyote Canyon and traveling toward the south, the first tributary canyon from the west is Parks Canyon, getting the name because of Ike Parks having a camp there during a dry winter when the Parks family took cattle into the desert area to try to keep them alive. The next tributary canyon from the west is Alder Canyon, known to some as Elder Canyon. Then the tributary canyons to the west of Joel Reed Valley are: Thousand Palm Canyon to the west of Monkey Hill, Sheep, Cougar, and Indian Canyons to the west of the main part of the Valley.

Cougar and Sheep Canyons I know nothing about, for the cattle did not use them, but I have been in Indian and Thousand Palm Canyons when working with cattle. The farthest I ever went up Thousand Palm Canyon I had to go on foot to get around some Mexican steers that had wintered on the desert. These cattle climbed around in much rougher places than did the natives.

Coyote Canyon is one of the more historical areas of the Anza-Borrego Desert, and I never did learn from the old-times the origin of the name, but I have wondered if perhaps some of the first white men traveling through may have seen many coyotes that had migrated from the higher altitudes during the winter, or, the name could have come from the Indians, through whatever name they had for this cunning little animal.

Diarists and historians have recorded that Pedro Fagas traveled through Coyote Canyon in 1772, and that Anza traveled this route in 1774 and again in 1775. It is to the Anza Expedition that many places on the desert have lost the names known to the old-time cattlemen and prospectors.

Near the latter part of the 1870's or the very beginning of the 1880's, a man by the name of Vines was camped at Mangalar Spring to the northwest of Middle Willows, and to the southwest of Fig Tree, (Upper Willows), taking care of cattle he had in the Coyote Canyon. One day he rode his horse to an Indian camp on the west bank of the wash at the mouth of Horse Canyon and accused an Indian man of killing one of his cattle.

The Indian's name was Tomas Arenas, a fearless man, and the moment he was accused of killing a beef, Vines had gotten himself into serious trouble, so the fight was on. The Indian grabbed Vine's horse by the bridle rein with one hand, and with the other hand he had Vines by the leg. Vine's horse was very thin, so thinking to save the horse from carrying extra weight, he had no gun.

Vines was soon on the ground fighting with a butcher knife he was carrying, and it was not long until the knife had done great bodily injury to the Indian. Before long the Indian was dying from the knife wounds, so the struggle was over, and Vines returned to his camp where he remained until after dark.

While having time to think the situation over, he realized he was in a dangerous situation, and sound reasoning told him the Indians would be watching the trails leading from the area. When darkness came Vines decided the trail leading nearby the Indian camp would be the one they would least expect him to use in an effort to escape, so cautiously slipping out of camp on foot, and carrying his rifle, he started on his way.

There were two major reasons why Vines did not ride his horse. In the first place, the horse was so poor that it could not carry the weight of a man with any degree of speed, and then he could travel so much more quietly on foot and be much more difficult to identify.

During the night Vines arrived at Jim Hamilton's ranch at the foot of the mountain on the east side of what is now known as Anza Valley. Mr. Hamilton was known to everyone as "Uncle

Jim", well-liked by everyone, and Vines felt sure that he could borrow a horse to continue on his way to escape. Anza Valley at that time was known to the old-timers as the Cahuilla Plains, and "Uncle Jim" would sit on his front porch where he had a wonderful view of the entire valley, always watching for the dust of any traveler that might be coming his way. My father would stop there when going through with the ox team, and "Uncle Jim" when speaking of the oxen would say: "Quitman calls them oxen, but they are nothing but the wildest kind of steers."

When Vines left the Hamilton Ranch on the borrowed horse he rode hard to get by the Cahuilla Reservation while it was dark. Arriving at my father's parents' place just off the Reservation at the west end, he rode up to the house and called "hello", as many old-timers did instead of knocking on the door. After relating the trouble he was in, my father's brother, William, loaned Vines a fresh horse so that he could hurry on to Temecula.

A short time after Vines arrived at the Reed homestead and related his story, my father uncoupled his ox wagon and prepared two of the wheels to serve as a cart in going to Coyote Canyon to get Vine's camp equipment. He yoked two of his oxen to the two wheeled vehicle and started on his way through La Puerta. At that time La Puerta ("The Door") was occupied by the Indians, and later became known as the Fred Clark place when it was purchased from Pisqual as shown in these pages by a reproduction of the paper of transfer. For many years the place has been occupied by the Art Cary Family.

Getting down over the ridge that now bears the name of Anza was quite a task in those days, even with the two wheeled vehicle and the two oxen. My father related that the trip was uneventful other than getting over the very steep, rocky Anza Ridge, into Coyote Canyon and out again.

In the 1880's Joel Reed, who was a distant cousin to my father, established a squatter's right at the large spring that now bears the name of Santa Caterina. The spring and the surrounding land was a trouble spot for Joel over a period of many years. First a man by the name of Fain tried to scare Joel out of the Canyon by making threats. At two other times later on he had trouble with persons who tried to dispute his right to the spring and the land, saying he was wrong in the location and numbers of his land.

The man Fain had evidently been a troublemaker wherever he happened to be, for when a very small boy I heard old-timers talk about his way of conduct. Through notes and tape recordings I have from one of my mother's brothers (Judd Tripp), who is still living at the age of 86, I possess information that Fain came to California to live with an uncle after he got into trouble somewhere in the east. Sometime later, the uncle was found dead with a gunshot wound in the head. So suspicion arose that the nephew perhaps was guilty of the crime. The story goes that there was an Indian who could serve as a witness, and he was taken to San Diego for the hearing. Officers of the Law took the Indian to a hotel, but before the hearing could be held the Indian's body was found in a chicken house with a piece of rope around his neck. The story as told to me by Judd Tripp indicates that the Indian was the only possible witness, so there could be no indictment obtained at the hearing.

The homestead where Fain's uncle was found dead, was situated where California Highways 79 and 71 now join between Temecula and Aguanga. The shooting of Fain's uncle occurred about 1882, and Judd Tripp's father (S. V. Tripp) then bought the Fain homestead where members of the Tripp family lived for many years. Judd should be very well qualified to relate history concerning the man Fain.

On a tape recording I have from Judd, he relates another story concerning Fain. Judd tells of Fain's riding a mule to a ranch near Warner Springs where a shooting occurred between Fain and the rancher. At the beginning of the shooting, Fain was behind a tree that was not too large, and the rancher was shooting from the corner of his house. The rancher was hitting the tree so often that Fain became so nervous he left the place in a hurry.

The rancher then had Fain arrested, and the trial was held in Julian, California, at the saloon belonging to "Doc" Hopkins, who was Justice of the Peace. Fain hired a lawyer in San Diego who drove to Julian with horse and buggy to defend his client. The trial being held in "Doc's" saloon, it was convenient for the drinks to go the rounds during each recess, which evidently occurred quite often. After a time, Fain's attorney became rather loud and rough in the defense of his client. Judge Hopkins warned him several times concerning his ill-mannered courtroom conduct, but the warnings were much ignored until the Judge ordered the constable to throw him out of the courtroom. The constable, with the help of another man, took the attorney outside and tossed him over the hitch rail where patrons of the saloon and persons attending court tied their horses. The attorney was wearing a linen duster, and as he was tossed over the hitch rail, the duster was torn. Everyone then returned to the court room, the drinks again went the rounds, and the case was dismissed.

When Fain entered the court room he was wearing his gun, so the rancher objected to the Judge. The Judge stated that Fain was not bothering anyone, so he did not think it necessary that Fain be disarmed. As a young boy, and up into early manhood, I knew "Doc" Hopkins very well, and I thought of him as being a fearless man who could very well take care of his share of whatever situation might arise.

In 1912, I met a man in Imperial Valley, who as an officer at one time in Yuma, Arizona, had been in contact with the man Fain during some trouble he was in there, and he did not speak of the man as being one of any degree of true courage.

When Fain conceived the idea of scaring Joel Reed out of Coyote Canyon, he had misjudged his man. For Joel stayed with his claim, but carried a gun wherever he went. On March 21, 1889, Joel was at my parent's place in Reed Valley after he had walked out of Coyote Canyon to get some food and his mail. From my parents' place Joel was going to take a cart and horse to go to Radec to pick up whatever mail there might be for my parents or for him.

The Radec Post Office was on the old Fain homestead I have mentioned before, where Highway 79 and 71 join between Temecula and Aguanga. The Post Office came by the name Radec when Samuel V. Tripp (my mother's father) made application for the Post Office and gave the name Cedar. There was already a Post Office in the state by the name of Cedar, so Cedar was spelled backward and became Radec.

When Joel was ready to leave in the cart to go after the mail, my brother, Leonard, who was then a little boy of six years, asked to go with Joel, and his parents told him he could. On the way, a gust of wind blew Leonard's hat from his head, and when he jumped from the cart to get his hat, the double barreled shotgun Joel was carrying because of the trouble with Fain, fell from the cart, discharging both barrels, hitting Leonard in the neck and killing him instantly. This accident of course, was a terrible shock for Joel, and I have heard my parents say that they never saw anyone suffer such grief. I know of no one who ever heard Joel mention Leonard's name after this accident which occurred while the little boy was in his care.

When the time was coming near for Joel to make final proof on his homestead rights in Coyote Canyon, he asked William Tripp and Frank Hamilton to go down to look over his improvements so they could serve as his witnesses. While they were walking around looking over the place with Joel, three shots were fired from a rocky point to the southwest, the bullets kicking up the dust not far

Leonard Reed, brother of the author, was killed at the age of six by an accidental shotgun blast. (Lester Reed collection)

Quitman Reed, (standing) and Joel Reed. The latter established squatter's rights in Coyote Canyon in the 1880s. (Lester Reed collection)

from their feet. Hamilton and Tripp hurried to get cover behind a nearby bank, and when they looked back, Joel was still standing where he was when the shots were fired, evidently trying to locate the one who fired the shots, so that he could help out in the shooting. They called to Joel that he had better get under cover, and he leisurely walked over to where they were still trying to locate the person who had fired the shots.

Of course, there was no way of proving who fired the three shots, but it all lined up with the threats Fain had made to Joel. However, Frank Hamilton and William Tripp served as witnesses for Joel, and the lands were patented to him November 3, 1891.

After Joel received patent to his land in Coyote Canyon, he moved to some land adjoining my father's homestead in Reed Valley. Joel's new claim joined my father's land on the south and he ran water from the creek in a small concrete ditch to the best part of his land and developed a nice apple orchard and place to grow

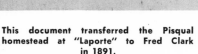

This document transferred the Pisqual homestead at "Laporte" to Fred Clark in 1891.

The second Joel Reed Cabin on his Coyote Canyon homestead. (Photo by the author, 1957.)

garden. Quite some time later, Joel learned from some of his friends that a family had moved into his valley in Coyote Canyon and disputed his right to the land and water there. This of course caused Joel to go back to his place in Coyote Canyon, and it was quite some time before the situation was cleared up. It was from this situation that new-comers in the area started the name of Collins Valley.

Another dispute came up over Joel's right to his land and water in 1922, and records show that Joel filed protest June 2nd of that year. I took Joel to San Diego to see his attorney during this dispute, and some time later he sold his land and moved back to Mississippi his home state, where he lived until he passed away.

In the early months of 1958, I spent some time in Coyote Canyon on horseback to refresh my memory concerning some of the old Indian trails and their village sites. When riding in the vicinity of Middle Willows, I saw for the first time, some palm trees growing in the willow and mesquite thicket. Right near thirty years had passed since I had been in the area, and it is possible the palms were growing then, but were not tall enough yet to show above the other dense growth.

CHAPTER 8

INDIANS OF ANZA-BORREGO DESERT

WE OFTEN hear mention of the pioneers of the Anza-Borrego Desert, and at such times, my foremost thoughts are of the American Indians and the still remaining evidences that they lived in these desert lands—for no one knows how many centuries before the white man interfered. Over some of the lower ridges, and through some of the more mountainous areas of the desert, there can still be found evidences of the network of trails over which they traveled for various reasons involved in their primitive ways of life. Along some of these trails there are still to be found small pieces of broken pottery indicating that perhaps such travel-ways were used when carrying water to some dry camp where they would be staying while gathering foods that no doubt would be carried over the same route to some of the main village sites.

Usually, on the higher ground near permanent water, and at times where there are indications that water was available during the rainy season, one can still find the metates (holes in flat-top boulders or rocks) made and used by the Indians for the grinding of some of their foods. Pictographs (Indian paintings) representative of their era are still intact on some of the more or less sheltered sides of some of the larger boulders. Occasionally, an Indian olla (specimen of pottery) may be found in some unexpected place on the desert. Around the village sites and burial grounds an occasional arrow-head, bead, or other specimen of interest may be picked up.

Throughout Coyote Canyon there remains much evidence that the Indians used this area extensively in their ways of livelihood. At La Puerta (San Carlos Pass), known to the old-timers as the door to the desert, there is much evidence of there having been a sizable Indian Village. The cold spring from which Fred

Indian metates at the Art Cary ranch at La Puerta in Terwilliger Valley.

Clark carried water for many years, over a distance of more than a quarter of a mile to his adobe house, perhaps was the principal factor in the location being a suitable village site. A short distance to the east of the spring is a hill upon which there are many huge boulders where the Indians no doubt found a certain degree of shelter. On the top surfaces of some of the more or less flat-topped boulders are numerous metates, and in some of the cave-like places among the boulders are pictographs.

Along the sides of Coyote Canyon where the flood-waters have not reached, there are signs of the mescal (agave) pits where the Indians cooked the base of the mescal stalk for food. The cooking process was accomplished by placing fair-sized stones in a circle several feet across, and then building a fire inside the circle to thoroughly heat the ground and the stones. The pieces of mescal were then placed within the prepared space and covered with hot rocks and dirt, and left to cook for about two days and nights. Jim Wellman and Lincoln Hamilton of the Anza area, sometimes still prepare mescal in this manner, and it was from them and Tiofla Helm of the San Felipe area that I learned something about the Indian method of preparing mescal for food. No doubt these men have always had matches to use in starting their fires instead of the methods used by the Indians down through the centuries. The remains of many of the old mescal pits tell the story of their having been used many years ago.

At Middle Willows in Coyote Canyon there is evidence of a sizable Indian village. On a ridge just to the south of where most of the water rises, there is a jumble of huge boulders beneath which there are many caves of surprising space. From these caves have been taken more specimens of Indian pottery than any other spot I know of in the Anza-Borrego Desert.

One spring, during the latter part of the 1920's, when we were gathering cattle out of Coyote Canyon to take them back to the mountains, a snow and rain storm came up, so we laid over a day at the Fig Tree (Upper Willows) Cow-Camp. To kill time, we went down the caves at Middle Willows to hunt for ollas, and one of the boys found three small ones. One of these ollas had a small opening at the top, and in the opening was some kind of hemp-like material tightly packed, then three flat pieces of rock were placed one on top the other over the opening, to serve, no doubt, in keeping out the rodents. Inside the olla were seeds of watermelon, pumpkin, muskmelon and sunflower. In with the seeds was a piece of wax-like material we thought had been placed there to serve as a preservative, for the seeds were apparently good, and we knew of no gardens planted in the Coyote Canyon area for many years.

At Mangalar Spring a short distance to the west and a little to the north of west of Middle Willows are some of the grinding holes in a flat rock slightly above the surface of the ground, indicating that the Indians used this spot, for the food grinding holes are deep and well worn.

In the Joel Reed Valley are evidences of a sizable burial ground and villages. To the west of the Joel Reed Valley, not far from the mouth of Indian Canyon, can still be seen the remains of what such old-timers as Joel Reed, Frank and Fred Clark, Charlie Brown and others called the Indian Sweat-house. From what source they got the name I do not know.

There were a number of Indian trails leading from Coyote Canyon. One, up Horse Canyon leading to the present Santa Rosa Indian Reservation, and a branch from this trail leading from the water in Horse Canyon across the mountain in a south-easterly direction to Hidden Spring, Clark Lake, and into the Rockhouse Valley areas. Along this branch of the trail are evidences of many of the mescal pits.

An Indian trail up Nance Canyon to La Puerta is the one over which Frank and Fred Clark drove their cattle for many years, to and from the desert. The last time I was on this trail, the mesquite and other growth so overlapped the trail that it was difficult to follow.

Through Tule Canyon was another trail over which the old-time cattlemen traveled when hunting for cattle in the area, but was not used by them as a regular drive way. In early days the Tule Canyon Trail was a likely place to find where a mountain lion (cougar) had traveled through, and one time when Jim Wellman was riding the area looking for the signs of lions, a tiny little fox terrier that was running along ahead of him started barking, and when Jim arrived where the little dog was making such a fuss, an adult female lion was up a tree staring down at the little terrier as if the cougar were very thankful to have got out of reach of this vicious animal that had pursued her. All that any dog need do—regardless of size—to tree a mountain lion, is to run after it barking.

To the west of Fig Tree (Upper Willows) is a tributary to Coyote Canyon known to the old-timers as Alder (Elder) Canyon, and here can be found more evidence that the Indians lived there in the past. From not too far above the mouth of this canyon, an old Indian trail turns to the left and follows a ridge for quite some distance, then through some small sage flats, over ridges and through small canyons to Lost Valley, and then to the Warner Springs area.

From Mangalar Spring is one of the Indian trails leading to Middle Willows. From Middle Willows leading to the south through a flat area, and then on through a saddle of a desert hill is another short trail that brings one out into the mouth of Thousand Palm (Salvador) Canyon.

Leading from the Joel Reed Valley is an Indian trail going up Indian Canyon for quite some distance, and then across the mountain to the San Ignacio Indian Reservation, over which the Indians and their cattle still travel to and from the desert. Along this trail as one travels up the canyon are several of the Desert Palms (Washingtonia) growing along the way and on the side of the mountain to the right, and after the trail leads one along the side of the mountain after leaving the canyon, you can see palms and the redshank brush growing side by side. This is the only place I have ever seen the palms and redshank growing in the same spot, so perhaps it could be said that this is one place where desert and the mountains meet.

Calistro Torte was born at Hidden Spring. He was one of the last Indians to live in Rockhouse Valley. (Photo by author)

Pat Cassero, an Indian Cowboy who rated with the best. He worked right into his 80s. (Photo by the author)

From Middle Willows across the rugged mountain to the east is another one of the Indians' travel-ways leading to Hidden Spring, and in early days this trail was used by prospectors when in search of mining possibilities and to work their claims. Along this trail after one travels across the rough mountain, there is considerable evidence of the Indians having lived there, at least when gathering food. Near the larger granite boulders can be found small pieces of broken pottery and sign of the mescal pits.

A trail leading from near the mouth of Coyote Canyon to Hidden Spring can still be followed; starting up North Canyon (Box Canyon) for about a mile, then up a small side canyon for about the same distance to where the trail turns sharply to the right across several rocky ridges, then into some little valley-like places where the water stands for quite some time after heavy rainfall. Here again is evidence of the Indians having taken advantage of times when water was available for their camps while gathering foods.

Near the mouth of Coyote Canyon is the Ocotillo Fence, where the ocotillos are growing in straight lines indicating that sometime in the past they served as an enclosure. Pat Cassero, a Cahuilla Indian, whose funeral I attended at the Cahuilla Indian Reservation January 29, 1960 told me when he was well up in his 80's, that he was informed when he was very young that the ocotillo fence was built by a Yaqui Indian who married a Cahuilla girl. Pat did not remember for what purpose the fence was said to have been built, but thought most likely as an enclosure for a garden. Pat said he did know that the older Indians did plant gardens in the Coyote Canyon area, for he remembered that his father (Isador) would go to upper Coyote Canyon to plant gardens in one of the tributary canyons—perhaps Parks or Alder Canyon.

As a boy, Patric Gerald Cassero attended school at Perris, California; at Arlington, California, and about four years in Phoenix, Arizona. However, the schooling and experiences away from the Cahuilla Reservation did not lure him from his horses and cattle, he was one of the better cowboys of the Cahuilla area.

Pat took care of cattle for my father before, or just about the time I was born in 1890, and throughout his life—even when he was well up in his 80's—he was much better with a rope than the average. Pat did not follow the type of roping we see at rodeos, but as a working cowboy he was among the very best. Until shortly before his death, I saw him helping Howard Bailey working cattle on the Cahuilla Indian Reservation, and he would go into Coyote Canyon to help Howard there.

Pat's mother (Antonina Cassero) lived to be a very old lady. Evidently no one knew just how old she was, but it was thought she was well over one hundred when she died in 1939. She was one of the last of the Cahuilla women to still be making baskets, and most any day when the weather was not too stormy, she could be seen out in the front yard working with the baskets as shown by the photo in these pages. There was nothing much would please the old lady more than to give her a sack of Bull Durham smoking tobacco.

Within the Borrego Valley there still remains evidence of the Indians having lived there much of the time. In the southern end of the valley is what some people now refer to as Metate Hill —a low ridge running pretty much east and west—where there was

Antonina Cassero, mother of Pat Cassero, was believed to be more than 100 years old when this photo was taken. She was an excellent basket maker. (Mrs Arthur Cary collection)

probably a sizable village. Most of the granite boulders or stones in which were the metates or food grinding holes have been moved away, but the places where the Indians cleared the small stones for whatever kind of living quarters they had are still plainly visible. Evidently, water was obtainable nearby at the foot of the ridge, for some of the early day cattlemen dug out shallow holes to water cattle.

In the southeast portion of Borrego Valley, where there are some small sand-dunes there has been found remains of a burial ground and village sites. Mrs. Eddie DuVall at the Old Borego Store has a very interesting collection of arrowheads, beads, and many other specimens of Indian artifacts.

From the west side of Borrego Valley up to the Warner Ranch area were two main trails that can still be followed as far as Culp Valley. The one leading from Hellhole and Palm Creek area was used for many years by cattlemen from Mesa Grande when they moved their cattle to and from the desert. The one leading from Tub Spring was not used so very much by the old-timers, for the Hellhole Trail served their purpose much better. The Yaqui Pass Trail leading more toward the south from Borrego Valley was used by the old-timers when moving on horseback or with burros. Portions of this trail can be seen at the present time when driving over the surfaced road that now runs through Yaqui Pass.

To the east of Butler Mountain (Coyote Mountain) is the old dry lake known as Clark Lake, getting the name from Fred and Frank Clark who had a well there in the 1890's for the purpose of watering cattle. Down through the past as cattlemen, prospectors, and then the homesteaders, prowled the Clark Lake area, quite a number of ollas have been found. Pieces of broken pottery, pictographs, metates, and other findings indicate that the Indians did live there a lot, at least whenever water was available. Speaking of water being available reminds me of the winter of 1926 and '27 when Joel Reed and I watered our saddle horses quite a long distance back in the brush from what is the barren lake bottom. No doubt, as time went on down through the centuries, the Indians took advantage of such conditions, and could stay nearer to the available food in the area.

To the north of Clark Lake at the foot of the very rocky mountain, there were pictographs which I was fortunate enough to get photos of before they were messed up by vandals. The photos I have are just as the Indians made them, and were not messed up with chalk or paint with the idea that they would make better photos.

One winter during the latter part of the 1920's when we had a cattle camp at Clark Well, I was running a few traps in the sand-dunes to the north of Clark Lake where I expected to catch a few of the little desert foxes, and while prowling around for fox sign, I found a metate that I wanted to carry out to keep. I found it rather heavy to carry very far at a time so each day when I checked my traps I would carry it until I got tired, and then drop it down until the next trip. By this method I finally got it to where I would leave the Model T Ford. I still have this nice specimen in my possession. The same year I found another extra nice metate when stuck in the creek with the Ford on the Joel Reed place, so I still have the two of them.

An Indian trail that is still easy to follow whenever it was not in the sand washes, leads into the Clark Lake area, with a branch leading to Hidden Spring. This trail comes across a rough ridge extending to the north from Butler Mountain, and was used by the Clark brothers when taking supplies to their cow-camp. This trail starts across this rough ridge directly across the valley from the Doc Beaty Place (Anza Ranch).

To me, the trail that is the most interesting of any that I know, is the one that starts to the east from Palo Verde Wash, across a very rough high desert hill, then into Smoke Tree Wash, and on across the Santa Rosa Viejo Mountain into the Salton Sea area. The first time I was on this trail, I went with Karl Bennis when he wanted to show me what the old-timers called sheep tanks, because of the Big Horn Sheep watering there after heavy rains when these holes in the boulders are filled with water as the water runs down the canyons that have such places in the bottoms.

Karl had been to one of these sheep tanks about thirty years before; now, thirty years is a long while to be away from a place and still remember the exact location of a sheep tank in such rough and rugged terrain. However, when we rode our horses into Smoke Tree Wash, Karl said that it should be not too far to the location of the tank. As I sat on my horse—or mule, rather—I could see one of the Indian metates in the top of a large boulder, so I suggested that we ride to the top of a nearby hill to get a better view. As I looked across a canyon to the east of us I could see old trails running along the side of the hill and it was very reasonable to assume that these trails had been made by the Big Horn Sheep. The trails were all leading to the bottom of the canyon below us, so I left my mule and walked to the bottom of the very rough canyon, and there I found a tank of water just as Karl had described it to me. I then walked up the canyon and found four more tanks of water as had been reported by Ada Bouril, a friend of Karl's whom he had directed to the location of the tank he had seen. Karl Bennis at the time was a man 82 years young, and I told him I would be willing to gamble that he was the only white man of 82 years who had ever ridden a horse over the rough Indian trail leading to the location of the tanks. When Karl directed his friend Ada to the location of the tanks he was then far enough past 21 that he felt he did not want to try walking from where they had to leave the jeep, so Ada, who is well experienced on the desert walked on to her successful find.

Going to the water tanks with Karl aroused my curiosity to learn more about this old Indian trail, and the points to which it led. Some time later, I rode my mule over this trail, and found what were to me many things of interest.

After the trail leads to the side of the mountain on the east from Smoke Tree Wash above where the sheep tanks are in the side canyon, I found another small tank of water from which I watered the mule. Not far from this water tank, there are signs of there having been an Indian camp. The spots they had cleared for living quarters are still visible, and the stones and charcoal of the mescal pits are still there.

Karl Bennis with some of the Indian relics found in the Anza-Borrego area.

After passing over the main ridge of the Santa Rosa Viejas, there is a small cotton-wood tree growing in a small canyon to the north of the trail where there are signs that the Indians had water for a camp during some of the more rainy seasons. As I traveled farther along the trail toward the east, I found two piles of small stones beside the trail; persons who should know tell me they had something to do with Indian ceremonials. However, I never have talked with any of the Indians about this.

Farther along the trail are again signs of an Indian camp, and a trail leads from this camp-site to a place in a canyon nearby where they no doubt obtained what water they needed. A little farther along the way are some metates indicating they had been used many times, and no doubt over a period of many years.

The trail then leads into one of the larger washes that runs past the Wonder Stone Hill, and perhaps this solves the mystery of why pieces of wonder stone have been found in Coyote Canyon and other places on the desert. After so many years of the old trails not being used, it is difficult to tell much about their exact course along the washes, but there can be little doubt that this trail was one of the main travel ways to the Salton Sea area, where of course there still remains signs of Indian habitation.

The author at one of the sheep tanks in the mountains that surround The Borrego Valley.
(Ann Wissler photo)

I have hoped that in the very near future the Park Service would start the idea of doing maintenance work on the trail I just mentioned, along with the one leading from North Canyon (Box Canyon) to Hidden Spring; the Hellhole Trail from Hellhole to Culp Valley, and the one from the Doc Beaty Place to Clark Valley. I do not mean to work them with modern machinery, but to clear the rocks from them by hand tools, so as to preserve these travelways as near as possible to the way they were when the Indians used them. This, no doubt, would encourage persons who like to hike, and those who like to ride on horseback to use these old trails, and the use of them would tend to keep them so that they would be easy to follow.

A few miles to the east of Clark Lake, and in a canyon well up in the mountains to the north of Palo Verde Wash, is what is now known as Rattlesnake Springs. This is a permanent water, and here again is evidence that it served the Indians well as one of their villages or camps. Here again, as appears to always be the case, the camp site was back away from the water, which perhaps had something to do with their respect for wildlife. This spring was not named by old-timers as was Joel Reed Valley, Monkey Hill, Butler Mountain, Hellhole, Yaqui Well and other places in Anza-Borrego Desert Park. This spring was named by Doc Beaty, Vermal Clark and Jim Wellman about the year 1917, when they were prowling around on foot and went to the spring to get a drink of water. Doc Beaty arrived at the spring ahead of Vermal and Jim, and finding a rattlesnake there, he decided to tie it in the trail where Jim and Vermal would come to get a drink. Perhaps this could be considered as a joke a bit on the rough side, but nevertheless, the snake was tied in the trail with a string, and resulted in the spring getting the name it bears today.

In the vicinity of Seventeen Palms and the Old Borrego Spring, short strips of the old trails can still be found, but cannot be followed with any degree of success because they followed the washes in most places where the floodwaters and blow-sands have caused the old trailways to disappear.

To the north of Clark Lake, and beyond some very rugged desert hills is the Rockhouse Valley that extends for about three miles to the base of Santa Rosa Mountain—mainly the Toro Peak. In the Rockhouse Canyon to the south of the Valley is the Hidden Spring where Calistro Torte was born somewhere between 80 and 100 years ago. The old village site is to the west of the spring on a mesa considerably higher than the canyon bottom where the small spring seeps from the west bank of the canyon. Metates or food

Seventeen Palms, a desert watering place in the eastern portion of the Borrego Badlands. (Photo by Ann Wissler)

Borrego Badlands, a section of eroded mud hills. (Photo by Ann Wissler)

grinding holes, pieces of pottery, and signs of charcoal still mark the location of the village site.

Calistro is the last of the Indians still living whom I know lived in Rockhouse Valley, and at the present time (1963) he resides at a rest home in San Jacinto, California. His father's name was Manuel, and he was thought to be well over one hundred when he died. Manuel Torte was the chief of the Rockhouse Valley Indians, and portions of the rock walls of the Torte home are still to be seen in the southern portion of Rockhouse Valley where there are the remains of three other rockhouses—one of them the home of the Andreas family.

In the Manuel Torte family there were two sisters to Calistro, (Josephine and Susan), and two brothers (Julian and Salvador). Calistro worked with the surveyors for about nine months on the route for the Palms to Pines Highway that we now travel between the Santa Rosa Indian Reservation to Palm Desert on California Highway 74.

About one half mile to the east of the remains of the Torte rockhouse is a lone cottonwood tree, and nearby is the place where the Torte family and the Andreas family no doubt obtained their necessary water supply. This watering place is not what one could call a spring, but usually, the water is so near the surface that water could be available by digging a shallow hole. Coyotes, bobcats, foxes, a few wild burros, desert birds, and an occasional Bighorn Sheep are known to still water there during seasons when much rainfall comes in the area.

After white men interfered in the Indian way of life, the Rockhouse Valley Indians moved to what is now the Santa Rosa Indian reservation, and it was there that I became acquainted with the Tortes. Three of the Tortes—cousins to Calistro, I believe— were among the better baseball players of Southern California in their day. They were "Alex", Raphael and John, and they, I am quite sure, the same as Calistro, received their early schooling at Perris.

At the base of Toro Peak, in the northern portion of Rockhouse Valley, near a little spring of water are the remains of another rockhouse Indian village. In what is left of two of the rockhouses can still be seen evidence of the fireplaces. To the south of the little spring is a rock circle that is still very much intact, and even though this wall is circular instead of being made with four corners as all the others were, it no doubt was one of their dwelling places. A short distance from this circular wall is another wall with four corners that is still very well-preserved considering the number of years since it was used. There are other places at this

Remains of the Manuel Torte rockhouse in the Rockhouse Valley. (Photo by author)

Ocotillo fence supposedly built by a Yaqui Indian long ago.

village site that appear to have been used as places of habitation, even though there are no rock walls. The surface of the ground indicates that these spots were used to a great degree, and it would be my guess that brush houses had been there at one time.

During the summer of 1962, a descendent of the Rockhouse Valley Indians (Art Guanche) and a fellow by the name of Henry "Hank" Lichtwald developed the spring at this village site as a watering place for wildlife of the area. The development of this watering place was a part of the game management program of the California Department of Fish and Game.

At the base of Toro Peak, to the northeast of the main Rockhouse Valley, is a fine spring of water that rises from the east bank of the canyon. The spring is known as Nicolas Spring, and the canyon down which the water runs for quite some distance bears the name of Nicolas Canyon, getting the name from the last one of the Indians to live in the area—Nicolas Guanche. On a ridge to the south and east of the spring, are the remains of the old Nicolas rockhouse, and in a basin to the north and east of the site of the rockhouse is a row of cottonwood trees that were no doubt

Collection of Indian "morteros" belonging to Mrs. Marion Anderson of Ocotillo, California.

Two metates found by the author, one near Clark Lake, the other in Coyote Canyon.

Remains of the Nicolas Guanche rock house to the east of Nicolas Canyon, and southeast of a spring bearing the Indian's name.

Skeleton of an Indian hut found by Nina Shumway years ago. (Karl Bennis collection)

planted by the Indians. Along the side of the hill below the spring is evidence of a ditch through which the Indians probably ran water from the spring to water their gardens.

Alder trees grow for quite some distance along the bottom of Nicolas Canyon where the water runs from the spring, and in a small flat area on the west bank of the canyon there are metates in some of the granite rocks, and in one place on the sheltered side of a huge boulder are dim signs of pictographs. The signs of the Indians having lived here would indicate that this spot was used as a village site long before the building of the rockhouses in the area.

When very young, I remember seeing Nicolas Guanche riding an old sorrel mule, and Jim Wellman tells of the mule having a habit of bucking the old man off most any time he felt in the mood, and if the mule failed in his efforts, the old Indian felt there must be something wrong with the mule.

The nearest I have come to learning the date Nicolas passed away, is from Lincoln Hamilton of Anza who cannot give the exact date, but states that he knows it was between 1914 and 1921. Nicolas was buried in the little Indian cemetery just back of the small Catholic Church on the Santa Rosa Indian Reservation, at the west base of Santa Rosa Mountain.

Art Guanche, a grandson of Nicolas Guanche, still resides at the Santa Rosa Indian Reservation with his mother, Louise. A brother, Joe, resides at Soboba Indian Reservation so his children can attend the San Jacinto schools.

Ignacio Guanche, the son of Nicolas Guanche and father of Art and Joe, was a natural violinist who studied music when going to school, and I never have known anyone whom I thought could get such sweet tones from a violin. Just about two weeks before he passed away March 9, 1923, I was at the home of John Torte on the Santa Rosa Reservation to stay for the night. John and I walked across the valley to visit with Ignacio, and we had been in his house a very short time when he suggested that we play the violin and guitar.

When midnight came, Ignacio had no thought of having played long enough, but I had left my home about twenty or more miles away at 2 A.M. that morning on horseback to gather cattle at the reservation, so I told him I would have to have some rest for my work the following day. Ignacio wanted to learn an old-time waltz I played of which I never did know the name; it would be impossible for me ever to play the waltz again without thinking of him. I promised Ignacio I would be back to play all night.

Louise Guanche, the wife of Ignacio, is the daughter of Hypolite Escallier who came from France at the age of 17, and was an early settler between Aguanga and Oak Grove on California Highway 79. When I was a very young man, Hypolite drove two horses to a spring wagon as the mail carrier between Aguanga and Temecula.

About the first of this year (1963), Ann Wissler of San Bernardino presented Louise Guanche with a statue of Saint Ann for the little Catholic Church near her home, and that evening when I stopped in to see Calistro Torte in San Jacinto and told him about the presentation of the statue for their little church he appeared to be very much pleased about it, and said that he expected to be at the church that night for some religious ceremonial.

Of the old Indian trails leading to and from Rockhouse Valley is one between the present Santa Rosa Reservation and Nicolas Canyon that is still used by persons going to or from Rockhouse on foot or on horseback. A branch of this trail leads to or from an old village site well up on the side of Santa Rosa mountain where for many years there were several of the Indian ollas that were never bothered by the old-timers, but in later years when the collecting of ollas and other specimens of the Indians' primitive way of life became of interest to many persons, the ollas disappeared from one of the adobe buildings where they had been for so long a time.

The old Indian trail between Hidden Springs and Rockhouse Valley is now visible only where it was not in the bottom of the wash (which is not in very many places), but throughout the area short strips of the old trails can be found leading to the different village sites, and to some springs at the base of the Santa Rosa Vieja Mountain bordering on the east. One of the main trails leading to and from Rockhouse Valley was between one of these springs and Martinez Canyon on the east slope of the Santa Rosas, and no doubt this trail would be found very rough at the present time, for it is seldom used any more.

The old trail leading from Rockhouse Valley to the north on Toro Peak is said to be extremely difficult any more because of its not being used and due to heavy rains that have fallen through the years.

Back during the years of the 1870's through the 1890's Rockhouse Valley was respected by such old-timers as the Thomases, Hamiltons (Joe and Henry), Tripps, Parks brothers (Jay, Joe, Ike and Lincoln), Frank and Fred Clark, Manuel Arniaz, Frank Wellman, and Quitman Reed as a place where the white man was not very welcome. No doubt the Indians still living there at that time rightfully felt that the white man had already interfered too much in their homeland.

A white man on horseback who arrived in the Kenworthy
area was advised by some of these old-timers not to go into the Rockhouse Valley area, and some time later when he appeared traveling
on foot with a bullet wound in one leg, and his horse had been killed,
he was a much wiser man than when being advised to stay away
from Rockhouse Valley.

About four years ago, a jeep was driven into Rockhouse Valley by way of Hidden Spring—that is, by the use of a power other
than the engine and traction of the jeep. It was evidently hoisted over
the rocky bluff in the Rockhouse Canyon quite some distance above
Hidden Spring. I have not been in the Canyon recently to know
if other jeepers have followed the same methods to get into Rockhouse Valley. There is little doubt but that the days when Rockhouse Valley is not accessible to motor vehicles will soon have taken
a place in the history of the past.

The first time I was in Rockhouse Valley, Karl Bennis was
with me, traveling with saddle animals and pack mule. We were
traveling by way of the trail going in from the Santa Rosa Indian
Reservation, when we came to foot-prints and the tracks of a burro.
We soon found where the burro had been tied to a mangalar bush,
and when following the foot-prints away from where the burro had
been tied, we noticed that there was something peculiar about the
foot-prints of one of the two men, for there would be the print of
a man's shoe, and then where the print of the other foot should be,
we could only find the mark of something that came to a point not
more than the size of a fifty-cent piece. Paying so much attention to
the sign of those who had been in the area before us was something
new to Karl, and it was only natural that he wondered about it.
This, of course amused me, so when I noticed some bare-foot tracks,
I remarked there was a freckled faced boy in the party, and of course,
Karl then had very little confidence in my ability to read sign. We
went on to Nicolas Spring feeling sure that one of the men was wearing a pegleg, but we had no hopes that Pegleg Smith was again prowling around on the desert. Karl did not believe that I could see
freckles in the barefoot prints.

Upon arrival at the spring, I picked up a post card addressed
to Mrs. J. W. Bryant at Calipatria, California, and I then turned to
Karl and asked if he remembered the two men who came to one of
our camps near Calipatria and tried to sell me a hound dog. He
answered that he did, and I reminded him the one with the pegleg
was J. W. Bryant; he admitted he believed there was much that
could be figured by sign, but he wanted me to understand he had
seen nothing to indicate the barefoot prints were those of a freckled-
faced boy. When visiting places where this party had camped we

Indian grinding holes near Little Blair Valley, in the Anza-Borrego State Park. (Photo by author)

Indian pictographs on a rock at the foot of the mountain north of Clark Lake. (Photo by author)

found pieces of broken Indian pottery; when coming in contact with Bryant later on I learned that they had been in the area searching for Indian pottery.

I never have been in any area of the Anza-Borrego Desert where signs of Indian habitation could not be found. Even along the ancient shore lines of the Salton Sea can be found pieces of broken pottery, and arrowheads have been picked up by persons interested in gathering specimens of the ancient Indians' primitive ways of life on the desert. Wherever the mescal or agave grows on the rough desert hills remains of the pits where the Indians cooked this plant are still to be seen.

Today, when traveling toward the east on California Highway 78, and after passing Tamarisk Camp Ground, and looking toward the south, there are some low hills apart from the main desert range where there is sign of there having been some sizable Indian villages. The deep metates indicate that these village sites served the Indians' way of life for many years. The nearest water to these village sites known to white man today are the Yaqui Well to the west and what is now known as Blue Spring to the south at the base of Pinyon Mountain.

Short strips of the old trail between these village sites can still be followed, and a main trail led up Mine Canyon to a village site in Earthquake Valley where the many metates indicate this was a sizable village. Another main trail leads from the village sites to the south of California Highway 78 to Harper Flats to the east of Pinyon Mountain, and then on into Hapaha Flat where there is evidence of an Indian Village that must have been much larger than the average, for there are many metates in the large boulders, but today there is no known water within several miles.

However, across a small canyon where most of the metates are, deposits of clay cause one to wonder if there may have been clay dikes across the canyon that could have brought water to the surface. The first time I visited this village site I was again prowling around with Karl Bennis, and he showed me the remains of the Indian hut shown in these pages as being found by Nina Paul Shumway.

To the south of Hapaha Flat, and on the south bank of Fish Creek Wash above Split Mountain is indication of another sizable Indian village, but unlike the village at Hapaha Flat, water is known to be near the surface in the main wash a short distance away. In the vicinity of this village site are strips of the old Indian trails leading in several directions, with one of the main ones leading up Sandstone Canyon and across some ridges in the direction of Vallecito, Caliente, Palm Spring (Mesquite Oasis), and Canebreak Canyon.

Back in the Tamarisk Grove area along Highway 78 and to the the west up Grapevine Canyon there is plenty of evidence of Indian habitation. Along the north side of the canyon and not far from Angelina Spring the metates show to have been used a great deal and near where Grapevine Canyon and Sentenac Canyon join is more evidence of an Indian village. Across the wash not far away was one of their burial grounds.

In the lower portion of San Felipe Valley where the surfaced roads fork, leading to Warner Springs, Julian, Borrego Valley, and Vallecito, many specimens indicating a village site have been found during excavation work, and it was there in 1867 when my father's parents camped there on the way from Texas that they witnessed the Indians burning one of their dead.

An interesting personality and descendent of the Anza-Borrego Desert now resides at the Campo Indian Reservation near Boulevard, California. Her name is Adeline Elliott, and she is the great-granddaughter of Hermon Nejo who was born at Yaqui Well and lived there when the desert was still the homeland of many Indians. Adeline tells of her great-grandfather being one of the Indians who traveled on foot and carried timbers from the Cuyamaca Mountains to San Diego for the building of the San Diego Mission. Adeline Elliott knows many of the old Indian trails well, especially those to the south from Mason Valley that lead from the

Mrs. Adeline Elliott, a descendent of the Anza-Borrego Indians.

desert into the Laguna Mountains. She speaks of trails that lead to Thing Valley and to the Campo area. When telling of her experiences in the desert areas she often mentions Mason Valley, Vallecito, Caliente, Canebrake, Carrizo Canyon, Bow Willow and Mountain Spring.

Mrs. Elliott tells of an experience that perhaps would have been a bit rough on many of us who depend so much upon the automobile for transportation. One night when camping in Carrizo Canyon, her saddle mule that she had hobbled to give him a better break in getting a little something to eat, evidently got to thinking of home and pulled out up the steep rough trail, leaving Adeline to walk and carry a twenty-five pound baby over the steep rough trail that was about a half day's trip with a saddle horse.

Adeline Elliott during her early life lived near Julian, and like most any girl living on a ranch at that time, she learned to milk cows, break colts to ride, build fences, plant crops and many other chores belonging to ranch life. She has lived on the Campo Indian Reservation since 1913, and she writes a much better than average letter. The descendents of the desert Indians are no longer many in number, and perhaps they are not as happy a people as were those who lived on the desert before the White Man came.

CHAPTER 9

NELSON BIGHORN SHEEP

THE NELSON Bighorn Sheep still survive in small numbers on the Anza-Borrego Desert, and it was generally understood by the old-timers that Borrego Valley came to be known by the name from the time the first Spaniards passed through the area. It was thought reasonable to believe that these animals were numerous at the time, and perhaps a considerable number of them were seen. The word "Borrego" is defined as meaning a lamb not yet a year old, and the word is generally used by sheep-herders when referring to sheep in general. The word is also defined as meaning: Simpleton, a soft, ignorant fellow. However, at no time during my younger days when living among old-timers of the desert, did I ever hear the word used in any such sense.

Perhaps the Bighorn Sheep fell victim to the Indian hunters from the beginning of their time together in the desert areas, but it would be difficult for me to believe that this animal would ever have faced the possibility of extermination through the lack of better judgment from primitive man—the American Indian.

During the winter of 1958 and '59, while wandering around on horseback in the northern areas of the Anza-Borrego State Park, I saw eight of the Nelson Bighorn Sheep, and three of them were beautiful old rams. These three rams were feeding at the southwest edge of the Joel Reed Valley when first seen, but of course chose the rough mountain to the south as their direction of escape. They did not climb the side of the mountain so very far before stopping on top of a pile of large boulders. I then rode my horse out of sight to dismount and tie her to a desert willow; then I proceeded to keep out of sight while climbing the mountain side to see how near I could get to them. I finally approached to within about forty feet of them. I only had one exposure left in my camera, so took a photo of them when too far away, and at the final moment had no film to use.

By riding over all the area I could immediately after showers or rains, I convinced myself there were as many as 32 of the Bighorns in the area covered. I do not mean to say that there were only 32 sheep in the area, but while working for the California Department of Fish and Game for almost ten years, I learned how far wrong one can be if relying at all on guesswork when wishing to arrive at a reasonable estimate regarding animal populations. When trapping mountain lions for the State, there were persons who would act as if they wondered why the State had me employed for such work when I would not make a statement as to how many lions there were within a certain area. However, the longer I worked at hunting and trapping, the less likely I was to make a statement concerning animal populations, for I have experienced much more of over-estimation, than of under-estimation.

I am not at all concerned with any fear that the Bighorn Sheep will suffer any casualties because of the past series of dry seasons, for there are enough permanent watering places in the Anza-Borrego Desert to take care of the actual sheep population. The permanent waters of Coyote Canyon, upper portions of Palm Creek, other lesser canyons, Rattlesnake Spring to the east of Clark Lake, Vallecitos, Carrizo Creek—and there are other watering places —I have never known to go dry. There are holes in the bottom of rocky canyons that fill with water after heavy rains fall on the desert, either from thunder showers, or from winter rains as I have seen on the desert a number of times down through the years. When such watering places do fill, the sheep appear to possess what may well be referred to as an uncanny or mysterious way of knowing or finding such water. When these holes (sheep tanks) do fill as I have seen them, the Bighorn Sheep then have access to browse and other forage that has had a rest during season of lesser rainfall.

In the bottom of a tributary canyon to Smoke Tree Wash, and pretty well up toward the top of Santa Rosa Vieja Range, I know of six of the sheep tanks that hold a good supply of water for quite some time after heavy rains, and the old sheep trails leading to them tell the story of sheep watering there, over a period of many years. There are more of the tanks on the east slope of the Santa Rosa Viejas in the Palm Wash, and when there, I saw the sign of a female sheep having watered at one of the tanks, and she had one or two tiny lambs with her—I could not tell for sure by the sign if there were one or two lambs. Had I followed the sign out away from the tank for a distance, I could have made sure as to whether there was more than one lamb. Old-timers have told me of tanks to the south of the Narrows in San Felipe Wash where Highway 78 passes through. I have been to one of these tanks when it was dry, but never have been to one high up on the mountain that is said to be a place that will hold a good water supply. However, when prowling around on the desert, there have been a number of times when I saw sheep sign indicating they were on their way to the tank high on the mountain.

Since the Anza-Borrego State Park has been established, I have hopes that the Bighorn Sheep will better survive the thoughtless ways of man, and will remain in reasonable numbers so that every little while some camera fan will be fortunate enough to get a "shot" at one. I took some people (Ann Wissler, Mary Trenery and her brother, Joe) on a sheep hunt with cameras some time ago, and it was great to note the pleasure these people had when "shooting" sheep with a camera, and the finest part of it was the sheep were still there for the next camera hunter to "shoot".

Photos of Desert Bighorn Sheep by Elerd Mock.

CHAPTER 10

KARL V. BENNIS

KARL BENNIS was among the first persons to venture into Borrego Valley when driving an automobile by way of Grapevine Canyon, Yaqui Well, and then over the old dirt road leading from the Narrows of San Felipe Wash into Borrego Valley. This route is the one over which Joel Reed hauled the lumber and metal roofing for the cabin he built after the original one was burned down. To take these materials to his homestead, Joel borrowed two horses and a buckboard from my father, and traveled the long way around because the route over what is now known as Anza Ridge and down Coyote Canyon was then so rough it would have been very difficult.

When Karl made his first trip into Borrego he was driving one of the old Jackson cars, and he established his camp among the mesquites in the lower end of the Valley. The year was 1910, and Karl had come from Maine to California in 1897, intending to go to the Klondike where he expected to be with an uncle. However, the journey to the Klondike did not materialize, so the man from Maine soon learned to like the desert areas of California, and has spent much of his time in the Anza-Borrego Desert. During the years since Karl first became fascinated with the desert, he has become much more familiar with the area than most persons, and through his knowledge of the Anza-Borrego area, he has been of great help to personnel of the State Park Service and others who were in search of first-hand information pertaining to the many places with which he has become so familiar down through the years.

Karl was born in Sullivan, Maine, March 21, 1876, and the place came by that name from his ancestors on the mother's side of the family. During our war with the British through which

Karl V. Bennis

we won our independence, one of Karl's ancestors by the name of Daniel Sullivan had harried the British to such an extent concerning their blockade of the Atlantic Coast, that they sent a warship down from New York to capture him. The British surrounded Sullivan's home where they found him, took him as their prisoner, then burned the place, leaving the family homeless in the snow.

Not too long after coming to California, Karl was employed by the Clark sugar interests, and later became superintendent of their factory at Los Alamitos near Long Beach. During the time Karl was employed at the Los Alamitos factory, he rescued two men from a tank where they had become stricken with gas fumes. This experience left him afflicted with a severe case of asthma that has hampered him to this day. Since becoming afflicted by the asthmatic condition, Karl's love for the desert has served him well, especially during the winter months of the year when the areas near the coast are so foggy and damp.

In the latter part of the 1920's Karl spent some time during the winter, with my brother, Gilbert, in the old cow-camp on Palm Creek very near the present Park headquarters and the main Park Camp Ground. While there my brother Gilbert "Gib" told Karl about some of the desert people finding ollas, arrowheads, and other articles belonging to the Indian way of life on the desert, making special mention of the Middle Willows area in Coyote Canyon. It was through Karl's search for such specimens that many places in the Anza-Borrego Desert became so familiar to him.

The first time Gilbert and I met Karl Bennis, he was at the Ike Parks Ranch in Cahuilla near the Indian Reservation. After visiting with Karl for awhile, we were on the way to the Reservation to do some work with our cattle; one of us mentioned the man Bennis appearing to be a person whom we could take on a trip some time when we were going with saddlehorses and pack animals. Some time after, when deer season opened, we invited him to go with us to Martinez Canyon and Ebens Valley between Santa Rosa Mountain and Salton Sea. It is needless to say he belonged in the picture just as we thought he would, and since that time I have never missed an opportunity to be with him on the desert.

Being around the cattle-camps appealed to Karl, and he enjoyed taking his camp-car and going along with cattle drives. It so happens that he was along with the last cattle drive George Sawday made from Warner Ranch to Temecula, with the cattle to be shipped by rail before the track was taken up between Temecula and Elsinore. He drove chuck wagon for the last cattle-drive Ike Parks made from Cahuilla to Temecula, and was with the last cattle-drive Arlie Bergman made from Aguanga to Temecula.

Karl drove a car as chuck-wagon for Frank Clark when he brought a small herd of cattle over the "Doc" Beaty Road into Borrego Valley, and these were the last cattle to be driven into Borrego. The original plan for the bringing of these cattle to Borrego was to haul them by truck to the County Well to be unloaded there and driven to Borrego by way of Old Borrego Spring, but due to some heavy rains the old Kane Spring Road was too muddy. Instead the cattle were hauled to Truckhaven and unloaded there. The rains had washed out the "Doc" Beaty Road so that Karl got stuck with the car he was driving as chuck-wagon; the equipment had to be unloaded and the car pulled out with the saddle horses.

Nearing the age of 87 in 1963, Karl Bennis lives in Temecula, and still drives his jeep wherever he wishes to go on the desert. I am looking forward to a time when he and I can again enjoy being together in our old stamping ground.

CHAPTER 11

"DOC" BEATY

"DOC" BEATY was the Borrego Valley homesteader who blazed the way for those who made their first trips into Borrego Valley by way of automobile. With mule-team and Fresno Scraper, "Doc" built a road from the Narrows in San Felipe Wash where Highway 78 is now graded into the side of the canyon wall; "Doc's" road led from the narrows over a short grade onto a mesa in a northwesterly direction to the main basin of Borrego Valley.

Not too far from the present location of the Borrego School was the piece of land "Doc" referred to as his homestead, but all during the time that I knew him he lived near the mouth of Coyote Canyon on what now bears the name of De Anza Ranch, and it was there that "Doc" always held open house to those passing his way.

One time when my brother "Zeke" was passing through Borrego Valley and Coyote Canyon on horseback from Imperial Valley he stopped at "Doc's" for the night, and after he had enjoyed a meal from the roast that was on the table, "Doc" remarked to my brother that he would bet he did not know what kind of meat he had so enjoyed after his long ride from Brawley. "Zeke" thought he knew what kind of meat it was, but realized he was wrong when "Doc" took him to where he had butchered and showed to him the hide, head and hooves of a wild burro.

During the depression days, the wild burros of Anza-Borrego Desert became a source of food supply for some of the people who had settled in the area, and for quite some time now the only wild burros I know of anywhere near Borrego Valley are only a very few in the Rockhouse Valley and Hidden Spring areas. I may have sometime enjoyed a feed of burro meat not knowing what it was. I do know that I had a big feed of raccoon and sweet potato after a long day's horseback ride without lunch, while staying for the night at "Doc" Beaty's with Frank Clark.

My brother "Zeke" worked with mules and Fresno Scraper to build the dam to make the reservoir just to the west of where "Doc" had his house on what is now known as De Anza Ranch.

"Doc" ran the Coyote Canyon water in ditches to the reservoirs near to his house, and irrigated trees and garden on the flat there. He had visions of using the water quite extensively on the mesa to the south of his house.

When "Doc" moved onto the De Anza Ranch, he and Joel Reed became not too friendly concerning the water rights in Coyote Canyon, so one time when Joel went from his place in Coyote Canyon to our home in the mountains about sixteen miles to the southeast of Hemet, he had some marks on his face that caused me to ask who he had been whipping. Joel's answer was: " 'Doc' and I tangled the other day and I took second place".

Even though "Doc's" likes and dislikes were far apart from mine, I told Joel that if the time should ever come when he needed help, I would be willing to bet that "Doc" would be one of the first to go to his aid. During the winter of 1926 and '27 when the flood waters poured out of Coyote Canyon into Borrego Valley in proportions that are difficult for many to believe who have not witnessed such situations, it was "Doc" Beaty who became concerned about Joel and went up to his place to see about how he was faring with such streams of water running past his cabin on two sides. "Doc" had to travel an old Indian trail to reach the Joel Reed Valley, and when he came to the bank of the stream to the south of Joel's cabin, Joel was out in the yard wondering just how much higher the water might get. A large sycamore tree had fallen across the stream, so by using the tree as a bridge, Joel was able to get across and go home with "Doc" for the night. At the time I was camped at the Clark cattle camp in Borrego, and I reminded Joel that it was "Doc", not I, who was thoughtful enough to go to see how he was faring.

Beaty, along with other interested persons, one time planted some trout in Coyote Creek, and afterward when the trout would be mentioned as having been seen in the stream, Joel would speak up and say that he had not seen any trout. My brother "Zeke" and Vermal Clark caught some of the trout and cooked them at Joel's place, and after Joel had eaten his share, the boys then asked what he thought about there not being any trout in Coyote Creek. Joel answered: "They didn't taste like trout to me!"

In later years, when Borrego Valley was getting pretty well settled up by homesteaders, and the cowman's day was just about over in the area, it was "Doc" Beaty who built the road from Borrego Valley across the northern edge of the Borrego Badlands to Truckhaven on Highway 99 not too far from the west shore of Salton Sea. Beginning in Borrego Valley, the "Doc" Beaty Road leads from the Pegleg Monument to the east between the Santa Rosa

Frank Clark (left) and "Doc" Beaty (center) take a prospecting party into Coyote Canyon (Howard Bailey collection)

Viejas and the badlands where it passes not too far to the north of Seventeen Palms.

At the point not far to the north of Seventeen Palms, where the first steep grade on the Beaty Road leads from Arroyo Salada, is the site of one of Beaty's base camps, and it is there that the Beaty construction party stored their perishable foods in a cave in the side of one of the mudhills that became known as Beaty's Icebox. However, the Beaty Road never did become a main traveled road, but is a good route for jeepers to travel when wanting to travel on one of the more out-of-the-way routes.

"Doc" Beaty, along with Ed DuVall, John Hilton, Harry Oliver, and Harry Woods conceived the idea of building a monument as a memorial to Pegleg Smith whom many an oldtime prospector of the deserts believed had found great riches of gold somewhere in the Anza-Borrego Desert. Down through life since a very young boy, I have overheard many discussions concerning the lost Pegleg Mine, so taking into consideration the many places referred to in these discussions, Pegleg Smith covered a lot of country in the Western United States. As far as I know, there is no one who can be certain the Pegleg Mine has ever been found. However, an uncle of mine (Judd Tripp) who is now on his way to the 87th birthday, believes that if the Pegleg riches ever have been found, the place was somewhere in Nevada.

"Doc" Beaty is known to have first come into the Borrego Valley area about 1909, and Arthur Cary who still resides on the old Fred Clark place at La Puerta (San Carlos Pass), along with his brother, Roe, of Oregon, tell about their father, Noah Cary, moving "Doc" Beaty's belongings from Mecca, California, into the Borrego Valley. Evidently, this was some little time after "Doc" had filed on the land he had chosen for his homestead.

The information I have states that Noah Cary of Thermal contracted to haul "Doc's" belongings from Mecca to Borrego Valley with four-horse team and wagon. At the time Noah Cary left Mecca, he thought of his mission for "Doc" requiring about a week, for making the round trip, but after encountering the deep sands below Old Borrego Spring and the John McCain cabin, along with other sandy strips, in this old-time route of travel, about twice the time thought of in the beginning had elapsed before Noah returned to his home.

Due to the manner in which the wagon wheels cut into the deep sands, "Doc's" belongings had to be unloaded and reloaded a number of times in order to make the load light enough that the weight could be relayed over the sandy stretches of road. To have the necessary water for horses and camp needs under such an adverse situation was quite a problem, and perhaps we of today after so many years of traveling over surfaced roads in cars, would be very much at a loss in knowing how to plan as did those who blazed the way with wagons, teams of oxen and horses, saddle and pack animals.

"Doc" Beaty came to know and use many of the old Indian trails in the vicinity of Coyote Canyon, Borrego Valley, Rockhouse Valley and the Santa Rosa Viejas. As I have stated at another place in these pages, it was through the wanderings of "Doc" Beaty, Jim Wellman, and Vermal Clark that Rattlesnake Spring became known by that name. Parts of the old pack boxes and other evidences of "Doc's" wanderings can still be found at some of his camping places, or perhaps where he had some kind of accident with his pack animals along some of the rough old Indian trails.

Today, as we sail along in our cars over the surfaced roads leading into the Borrego Valley, it is easy to forget that it was "Doc" Beaty with his mules and Fresno Scraper who blazed the way for us. I am quite confident that "Doc" gave credit to John McCain, the Clarks, the Tripps, Joel Reed, the Angel brothers and other Mesa Grande cattlemen, along with such old-time prospectors as "Dad" Hardy, the old colored man Howell and many other men with burros as being the ones who blazed the way for him in getting into Borrego Valley. These old-timers undoubtedly gave the Indians, and such expeditions as the Anza Party credit for being the ones who blazed the way for them when traveling in the Anza-Borrego Desert.

CHAPTER 12

MRS. MARION R. ANDERSON

MARION ANDERSON has been one of the more successful persons prowling the Anza-Borrego Desert in search of Indian pottery, and she possesses a fine collection of arrowheads along with some fine specimens of beads. At one time she had about forty pieces of pottery, and she still has a nice collection of metates and other such items of interest.

The first time I met Marion Anderson on the desert, I was on horseback in the Canebrake area with four or five young hound dogs following me. The young hounds were having their first experience chasing jackrabbits among the jumping chollas, and they had surely collected a full quota of thorns. The mess of thorns in the dogs did not appeal to Marion Anderson, so when she told me she was going to dethorn them, I felt that she meant it, and got busy catching and holding them for her.

The young hounds had never been petted by strangers, but they immediately became reconciled to the procedure of pulling thorns, and no doubt realized they had met with a sympathetic friend.

Marion Anderson has spent much time in the desert areas in companionship with Adeline Elliott (whom I mention at another time in these pages as being the great-granddaughter of the old desert Indian, Herman Nejo, who was born at Yaqui Well and was living there at the time he became one of the Indians who traveled on foot and helped carry timbers from the Cuyamaca Mountains to San Diego for the building of the Mission there.)

As desert companions, they have traveled over the old Indian trails leading into the mountains from Canebrake, Carrizo Canyon,

Bow Willow, and other places in that area of Anza-Borrego Desert. In telling of their experiences in these areas when hiking the old Indian trails, they often mention Thing Valley, the cattle camp in Carrizo Canyon, and make mention of the many places that still bear evidence of Indian habitations.

Marion Anderson knew of the old Indian trail that leads from Blair Valley across the desert hills to Vallecito. The first I knew of this Indian trail was in 1910 when cattlemen and other old-timers told of traveling it. At the present time, where the dirt road leads around the point of the hill from Blair Valley into Little Blair Valley, this old trail is visible from Blair Valley up over the hill to the south, and this portion of the trail as far as the top of the hill was used by the Marshall South family when living a rather primitive way of life in the area. This old trail route can still be followed except where the Indians traveled in the washes.

Marion Anderson tells of times down through the years before surfaced roads were the regular thing across the Anza-Borrego Desert, and says this old trail was used in the operations of those who smuggled Chinese into the U.S. She tells of having seen flashes of light along the trail at night that were thought to be a part of smuggling operations. I can well remember when I was a boy, I heard old-time officers of the law tell of picking up smugglers with Chinamen in the Warner Ranch, Oak Grove and Aguanga areas. Even after the Model T Ford came into the picture, and when I was traveling on horseback over the old dirt road between Hemet and Aguanga, I met a Mexican cowboy whom I knew fairly well, traveling at an unusual speed over the dirt road and looking back over his shoulder quite often. It was not long until I met some officers making better time than the cowboy, and in a few days I heard they caught the Mexican with a Chinaman.

Mrs. Anderson, with her late husband, for a number of years operated a gasoline station in Borrego Valley, but a few years ago they sold their business and moved to Ocotillo where Mr. Anderson became ill and passed away. Mrs. Anderson still resides at Ocotillo, and even though, she like myself, is quite a number of years past 21, she still loves the desert and takes advantage of every opportunity to prowl around in search of some specimen of the Indian's way of life. The finding of an olla has become a very remote possibility in most places. However, only a very few days ago, at the home of Howard Bailey and his wife Lola, Ann Wissler and I were shown a small olla they had found beside a trail they had traveled many times down through the years. Evidently, for years the olla had been hidden in a shrub beside the trail, but now that the bush had died the olla became visible to them, and added to the interesting collection of specimens from the desert in their new home on the old Frank Clark Ranch in Durazno Valley adjoining the Cahuilla Indian Reservations on the south. The possibility of such findings makes the pastime of hunting Indian ollas and other specimens still worthwhile to persons who appreciate the desert.

Mrs. Marion Anderson of Ocotillo, California, with some Indian ollas, grinding stone, and a basket from her extensive collection.

EARLY MORNING IN BORREGO

One early morning in Borrego, when the flowers were damp with dew,
I looked toward the Eastern sky, and saw the sun just peeking through.
From out toward Butler Mountain, came a coyote's lonesome wail,
And from a nearby mesquite thicket, I heard the call of Gambel Quail.

I could hear a desert roadrunner giving forth its mating call,
This call you do not hear in the winter, nor hear it in the fall.
I could hear another call from wildlife, one I most dearly love,
This call came from not too far away—that of the white-winged dove.

The desert fox had almost disappeared, as had the burrowing owl,
No doubt the heedless poisoners had recently been on the prowl.
Thoughtless persons had been collecting snakes, and other reptiles too,
Disregarding other people's interests, as thoughtless persons often do.

As I walked along this early morning, looking closely at the ground,
I saw the signs of Indians; broken pottery was scattered all around.
The Indians were the Borrego pioneers, with their primitive ways of
    life,
Perhaps happier than white men, with our mad rush of speed and
    strife.

I thought back to the days of the cowman, and his hardy desert cows,
Much of the range is now under irrigation, cultivated by the plows.
I remember when flowers were used as cow-feed, important in cow-
    man's plans,
Now these flowers are still important to the many camera fans.

Cowmen and prospectors were the old-timers of this arid desert land,
They were a rugged type of people, making the best of what lay at
    hand.
I knew many of these fellows, and was here when the homesteaders
    came,
The cowman's day was over, and life in Borrego will never be the
    same.

I thought of another morning in Borrego, not so very long ago,
When I rode up the Hellhole Indian Trail, an interesting trail to
    know.
I rode to the top of a hill, and sat for a long while on my horse,
I noted the change of Borrego, but not entirely with remorse.

I reminisced in fond memories of Old Borrego that meant so much
    to me,
I then surrendered my thoughts to New Borrego as rightfully it
    should be.
Down below me were camper's trailers, in the Anza-Borrego Desert
    Park,
A place for week-end excursions, on which many people now embark.

In view was the Christmas Circle, I could see gas stations, two or
    more,
A number of business places, the post office and grocery store.
Park Headquarters and the golf course I could see across the way,
It is a well-kept golf course and many visitors come there to play.

Again I wish to make mention of the Park Service, managed by
    courteous men,
Should you like the desert, visit with these fine fellows now and then.
Yes, I enjoy thoughts of Old Borrego and reminiscing into the past,
But time came for the transition, the cowman's day just could not
    last.

Now I accept the change in Borrego as the way for things to be,
I like to spend winter-time in this desert land, a delightful place
    to me.
I still love the early desert morning, the daytime and the hours of
    dark,
May God help to save our wildlife of the Anza-Borrego Desert Park.

By: LESTER REED

NORTON ALLEN

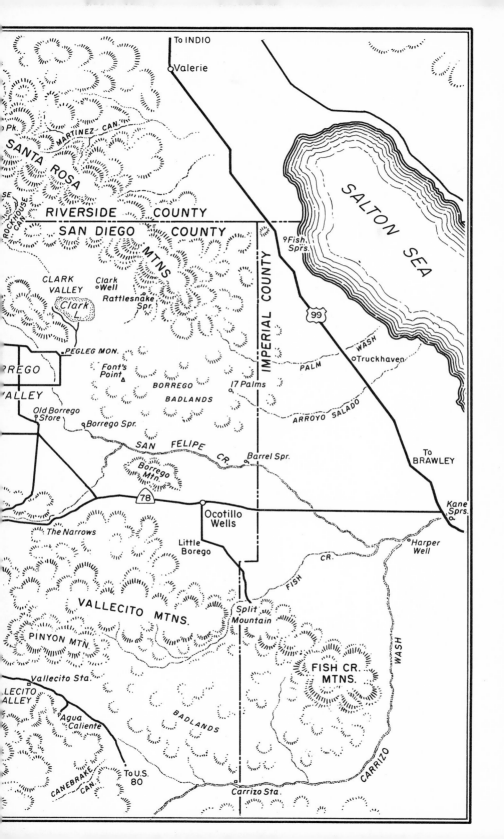